12
DAYS ON THE ROAD

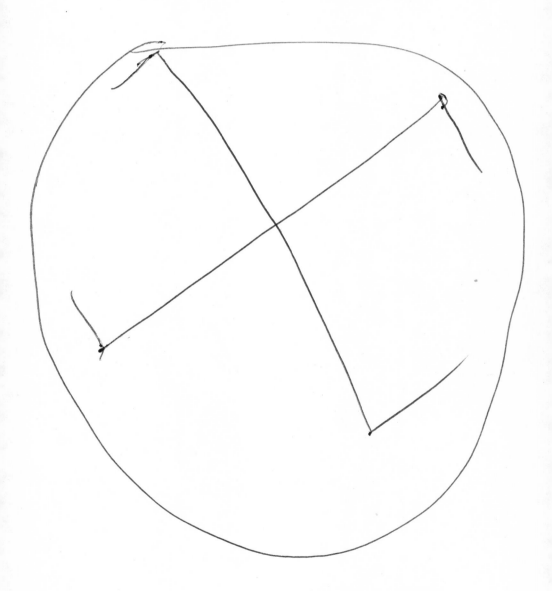

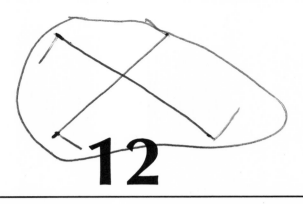

12
DAYS ON THE ROAD
THE SEX PISTOLS AND AMERICA

Noel E. Monk
and
Jimmy Guterman

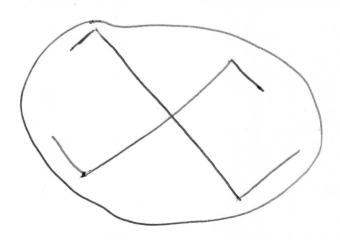

WILLIAM MORROW AND COMPANY, INC.
NEW YORK

Library of Congress Cataloging-in-Publication Data

Monk, Noel E.
    12 days on the road : the Sex Pistols and America / Noel E. Monk
and Jimmy Guterman.
        p.   cm.
    Includes bibliographical references.
    ISBN 0-688-09050-8
    1. Sex Pistols (Musical group) 2. Rock musicians—Travel—United
States. I. Guterman, Jimmy. II. Title. III. Title: Twelve days
on the road.
ML421.S47M66   1990
782.42166′092′2-dc20
    [B]   90-35920
                                                                           CIP

Printed in the United States of America

    2   3   4   5   6   7   8   9   10

BOOK DESIGN BY M. C. DEMAIO DESIGN

for
Janice S. Monk and Jane Kokernak

Acknowledgments

12 Days on the Road is the story of the Sex Pistols' tour as seen through Noel's eyes, but there are dozens of voices in this book. For giving us their time and sharing their memories, we thank Thornton Arnold, Dan Baird, Roberta Bayley, Jo Bergman, Doreen Cochran, Ted Cohen, Paul Cook, Bonnie Cupples, Norman Davis, Jim Dickinson, Roger Ebert, Bill Goffrier, Richard Gossett, Bill Graham, Bob Gruen, John Holmstrom, Penelope Huston, Rory Johnston, Bob Kelley, Howie Klein, Bob Merlis, Cindy Ornstein, Mike Peters, Jim Rink, Carl Scott, Bonnie Simmons, Barbara Skydel, Rex Weiner, and Will Wren, as well as the many who spoke with us off the record. A bit of information from a 1986 interview Jimmy Guterman conducted with John Lydon is also included in *12 Days*, although Lydon would not speak to us as part of the book research.

For their ideas, encouragement, and support, we thank Stephanie Campbell, Mark Caro, Charles Conrad, Kinky Friedman, Randall Grass, Pagan Kennedy, Dr. Barry Lieberman, Robert Linn, Milo Miles, Owen O'Donnell, Rob O'Regan, Oedipus, Tim Riley, Joe Rosenberg, Steve Schechter, Andrew Seidenfeld, Lydia Sherwood, Audrey Shulman, Murray Silver, Lauren Slater, Donald W. Spicer (as well as Andy McLenon and everyone else at Praxis International), and Tom Zutaut.

On the publishing side, we are grateful to Al Lowman

and Brian Moore at Authors and Artists Group, Jim Landis and Doug Stumpf at William Morrow, Susan Hill at Sidgwick and Jackson, Peter Laird, and Kerry Timbers.

Special thanks to John Hendel for specialty film processing, Photo Trend, Cypress, California.

Personal thanks to Speedy Dee, Big Ed, and the Kid.

Special thanks to Dan Baird and Doreen Cochran for giving us an anchor in Atlanta and to John Holmstrom for showing us the other side of the tour.

Special thanks to J.S.M. for driving us through East Pinhook.

Contents

12
DAYS ON THE ROAD

CHAPTER ONE

Across the Sea

SID VICIOUS'S FACE IS smeared with blood. Not all of it is his. The Sex Pistols have hit Texas, and Texas has hit back.

It's January 10, 1978. The Longhorn Ballroom in Dallas is packed, eighteen hundred strong. The air is hot and heavy as England's Sex Pistols conclude a thrash through "Holidays in the Sun," the most barbed, repulsive tale of a vacation ever put to harsh music. While Sid punches his bass-guitar strings with his wrist, drummer Paul Cook, stuffed into a white T-shirt that proclaims NEVER MIND THE BOLLOCKS, HERE'S THE SEX PISTOLS!, pushes his palms into the beat with the ferocity of a thug. To Cook's left, guitarist Steve Jones sprays sweat from his shaking forehead and jagged machine-gun chords from his battered, out-of-tune Gibson Les Paul. Frequently he lifts his right hand from his six-string to wipe audience spit off his face. He spits back just as often.

Sid breaks a bottle of Heineken over his bass amp, and opens a thin cut in the shape of a "U" across his chest.

In front of the drums, at the lip of the stage, singer Johnny Rotten crouches and glares at the crowd. His bright orange hair shoots out from his scalp in short spikes, and his cowboy outfit—fringed leather vest, white shirt, and black Wranglers, all brand new—is a parody of his southern audience. "Hel-lo, awl yew Cow-baws," he mock-drawls, enunciating each syllable like a measured threat. Finally, he tightens his sickly-pale face, and he screams.

"I don't wanna holiday in the sun! I wanna go to the new Belsen!" His cries bare his badly decayed teeth, which have earned him the Rotten monicker. "I'm going under the Berlin Wall! Please don't be waiting for me!" he signals the band to cut the song short right there, mid-chord, and Cook and Jones get the message. Vicious hammers his bass a few more times, and then loses interest. He remembers his nose is bleeding and wipes it with his right arm.

Most of the crowd tonight is made up of curiosity-seekers looking for a good time, but up front, pressed against the low wood stage, are hundreds of genuine, mean-looking, mean-spirited punks. The punks are barely one third of the crowd, but their energy overwhelms the thousand-plus gawkers. A teenage girl named Lamar who drove to Dallas from San Francisco just for this event, has spent much of the show trying to entice Vicious to lean down from the stage toward her. When he finally gets close enough, midway through "Problems," Lamar rears her head back and then slams it into Vicious's face, opening a gash on his nose. The blood mingles with his saliva as he spits into the crowd, then cradles his mouth in pain. Gabriela Gomez, one of Lamar's two traveling companions, flinches, fearful that Sid might hit back.

This is not what usually passes for musical entertainment at the Longhorn, a nightclub founded by western swing pioneer Bob Wills and managed for a time by Jack Ruby. Outside, overlooking the corner of Corinth and Industrial, a marquee illuminates the intersection with the strange combination: TONIGHT—SEX PISTOLS. JAN. 19—MERLE HAGGARD. Nine days from now, everything will be back in order, the sound of the cool Dallas evening filled with conservative country-and-western music and even more reactionary ideas.

"I just came to see the weirdos," boasts eighteen-year-old Keith Crawford. "I'd better get three-fifty worth of weirdos."

In Lamar, Keith may be getting his money's worth. A short blond punk, she wears a leather wristband ringed in barbed wire. She reels from the jolt of Sid's face, and enjoys it.

Noel Monk, the Sex Pistols' American road manager and Sid's de facto protector, moves toward Lamar to hit her back. Monk adjusts his baseball cap (which he's wearing to keep the crowd's spit off his head and face), and is about to backhand

Lamar, when Sid stops him. The pain has begun to subside, and the blood outlines a dopey smile.

"No, no!" Sid shouts in a Cockney accent. "She's OK. Leave her alone." Lamar and the other punks up front raise their fists and hoarse voices in solidarity.

Emboldened by their feisty support, Vicious reaches for his left arm, which was the subject of a self-inflicted attack a few days earlier. With blood trickling down his cheek and down his bare sunken chest toward his black jeans, he rips a pus-soaked bandage off the arm, revealing a deeper laceration. He throws the bandage into the crowd, and smiles wider while the devoted rip it to shreds, hungry for a special souvenir. He licks his lips, tastes the fresh blood, and smiles at Lamar. She points her middle finger at him.

Unamused, Rotten stares at Vicious's spectacle. He grabs his microphone, turns toward Vicious, stands rail-straight, and stares him down snidely.

"Sid-nay," Rotten taunts as his bass player upturns a new Heineken bottle and lets it mingle with his blood. "Whenever you're ready, Sid-nay." He speaks slowly, over-enunciating each syllable to emphasize his irritation. "These luf-ly cowboys would like to hear us purr-form."

Rotten signals Jones, who then unravels the repeated guitar figure that kicks off the vile kiss-off "Pretty Vacant." Cook's drums soon join in, and the punks up front jostle to the quick, quirky beat. Some of them pogo up and down, some of them slam against each other, dozens of them throw garbage onto the stage. Rotten shouts at the crowd, "You're so pre-tay! Oh so pre-tay! You're vay-cunt! And we don't care!"

The punks shout the words back; the put-down is all they need to have in common with the band they're spitting at. Behind the punks, a few dozen curiosity-seekers take the cue and toss whatever they can find toward the Sex Pistols. Onstage, four scraggly English kids are pushing out their music with as much anger and energy as they can muster. They play hard and fast, dodging the beer glasses, rotten tomatoes, pig snouts, and dirty Kleenex that serve as applause. This is nothing new; by now the foursome is resigned to the occasional outbreak of violence. They're deep in enemy territory.

*   *   *

Yet the Sex Pistols have been pulling up stakes in neigh-borhoods unwilling to house them since they coalesced. The Sex Pistols, the most controversial rock-and-roll performers since Elvis Presley and Jerry Lee Lewis barreled out of Memphis's Sun Recording Service two decades ago, the band that claims its goal is to destroy rock and roll, has worked in enemy territory from the start.

The Sex Pistols erupted out of London in 1975, offend-ing everyone from housewives and members of Parliament to the rock establishment, and inspiring hundreds of bands, with names like the Clash, the Buzzcocks, and the Damned, to scream as ferociously and obnoxiously as they could. The leg-end goes that not many people in England got to see the Sex Pistols because so many of their shows were canceled by the local authorities, but everyone who did get in started his or her own group. They all wanted to make a fun, dirty racket. The legend stretches the truth, but the truth is that people were inspired.

The music coming out of Europe's posh, antiseptic stu-dios in the mid-seventies was the essence of complacency, which Johnny Rotten and the Sex Pistols detested. Performers like Mick Jagger of the Rolling Stones and Rod Stewart, whose early work was infused with danger and excitement, had let their music and their ideas go to pot.

"I don't care what Johnny Rotten says," Jagger told *Rolling Stone*'s Chet Flippo. "Everything Johnny Rotten says about me is only 'cause he loves me 'cause I'm so good. It's true. . . . In a year, the Sex Pistols are gonna be *phffft!*"

As such a tirade suggests, the music of Jagger and his contemporaries sounded like that of tan, rich, pampered men. These entertainers had no interest in catering to anybody who didn't share the same cocaine-and-limousine life-style, or at least the desire to live it vicariously. (Rotten did pick up one thing from Stewart: his penchant for wearing plaid suits onstage. The only difference was that Stewart's suit pieces matched.) This laziness in rock reflected what was happening in England as a whole, with the privileged, divisive Tories about to come to power under the aegis of Margaret Thatcher, the party's Iron Lady. The very name Sex Pistols was a crude kick at the status quo; England was so sedated in 1975 it took a name like that to get noticed.

As provocative as Rotten and his lot were, naming the band the Sex Pistols wasn't his idea. In fact, the band itself wasn't his idea. For that, history will have to thank—or blame—a London entrepreneur/artist named Malcolm McLaren.

McLaren (née Malcolm Edwards), born in 1946, spent most of the sixties drifting through a handful of British art schools without direction; the only events of the time that certainly stayed with him from that time were the friendship he developed with budding graphic artist Jamie Reid and the 1968 attempt by the board of governors of Croydon College to get McLaren committed to an institution.

Wisely leaving Croydon behind him, McLaren arrived at Goldsmiths' College in 1969 and promptly began honing the concepts that would lead to the Sex Pistols. Inspired by his classmates and what he'd heard about the previous year's student riots in Paris, McLaren gravitated toward the pop art of Andy Warhol and the revived situationist theory of his fellow students. From Warhol, McLaren learned the power of subversive art; from the situationists, he learned the art of subversive power.

In the early seventies, McLaren saw himself as a failed fashion-boutique operator. With lover/partner-in-crime Vivienne Westwood he ran Let It Rock, an attempt to attract trend-obsessed latter-day Teddy boys. When that didn't work, he tried to pull in bikers by going heavy on the leather and rechristening the shop Too Fast to Live, Too Young to Die in 1973. In commercial terms the redubbed store was another dud.

In 1974, McLaren found his true calling, the ideal forum for his personal distillation of pop art, situationism, and carny ethics. When the glam-rock band the New York Dolls toured England late that year, their death knell grated even louder than guitarist Johnny Thunders's buzz-saw power chords. But McLaren had heard them, seen them (they'd showed up one day in Too Fast to Live, Too Young to Die), and he'd fallen in love with the idea of controlling an exciting, semicompetent, off-kilter, iconoclastic rock-and-roll band. Since no one in the

Dolls at the time was capable of arguing coherently, McLaren quickly became their de facto manager.

As he might be happy to tell you himself, McLaren's greatest single talent is for self-promotion, and the burnt-out Dolls were no match for his sensational ideas, like draping a hammer-and-sickle flag or a sign that read WHAT ARE THE POLITICS OF BOREDOM? behind the red-leather-clad band onstage. Within a few months, the band finally went under thanks to drug-fueled animosity (band members Thunders and Jerry Nolan were notable junkies), but by then McLaren knew how he was going to get rich and famous: rebel rock.

Years later, McLaren elaborated on this idea in an essay for *Spin*. "When I first heard rock and roll, I think it was 'Rock Around the Clock,' and that was back in the mid-fifties in England. The first time I saw a Teddy boy, it provoked in me sheer menace, so much that I crossed the road to get out of his way. The badness that it managed to promote made me love the clothes that this chap wore and helped make me understand that you could actually look bad—not be it. I realized fashion could provoke something that made you look completely out of step with everything else that people were terming good. In other words, you became an outsider. That made me fit in. The Sex Pistols was me when it was bad and something else when it was good. The color black, if it could be defined as a color, meant to me something very warm and very, very beautiful. The name came about by the idea of a pistol, a pin-up, a young thing, a better-looking assassin, a Sex Pistol. I launched that idea in the form of a band of kids who could be deduced as being bad. When I discovered that the kids had the same anger, could wear black, it was perfect."

McLaren returned to his shop at 430 King's Road, now called Sex, and further schemed to extend his romantic notions of blackness. Although the shop now catered to the bondage-and-titillation crowd and was finally making some money, the store's goods had nothing to do with the traditional idea of sex as shared pleasure. Its wares (mostly designed by Westwood, who was becoming increasingly estranged from McLaren) were intended to make its wearers look repulsive, even sexless; McLaren declared that his boutique expressed "the fashion philosophy of anti-fashion" and set out to define clothing style as aversion. With a few Sex shop regulars as willing stooges, he planned to do the same for pop-music style. (One shop worker he didn't get a chance to exploit before she moved on was a young American emigrée named Chrissie Hynde.)

Among the regular customers or shoplifters at Sex were Steve Jones, Paul Cook, and a buck-toothed guitar player named Wally Nightingale, all of whom had police records that ranged from petty theft to picking fights with bobbies. McLaren hitched the three of them (Jones, the man who stole most of the equipment they were using, was the ostensible singer) with Glen Matlock, a rudimentary bass player who worked weekends at the shop. The nascent group called themselves the Swankers. Wally soon disappeared on a wave of ennui and incompetence (nobody remembers what happened to him). Jones's dubious singing talent and relative shyness destined him to become a closed-mouth support guitarist, which left the group without a front man. So McLaren searched for the lunatic who would elevate them all.

That lunatic wasn't long in appearing. One day in the spring of 1975, a short, thin redhead walked into Sex. His posture suggested a hunchback-in-training, and when he opened his mouth his rotted teeth looked like open sores. Hanging off the chest of nineteen-year-old John Lydon was a pulverized Pink Floyd T-shirt. The graphic was razor-ripped, and the words I HATE were scrawled over the name of the band. The dollar signs went off in McLaren's head. Several pints of ale later, McLaren had convinced Lydon to lip-synch Alice Cooper's anthemic, "I'm Eighteen" in front of the Sex jukebox using a broken shower head as a makeshift microphone. He soon had the punter fronting the store's house band, the Sex Pistols.

Over the summer and fall, Lydon, now dubbed Johnny Rotten (for his teeth, of course, and, to a lesser degree, the rest of his body, which had been afflicted by a childhood bout with spinal meningitis), and Matlock (the only member of the band who considered himself any sort of a musician) collaborated on a group of fiery, madhouse songs that hammered simple anti-homilies into savagely efficient scorchers. McLaren encouraged them to be revolutionary and inflammatory, and his pupils didn't disappoint.

Lyrics spiraled out, grabbed a listener by the throat, and didn't let go. In "God Save the Queen," Rotten raved, "God save the Queen! She ain't no human bein'! There is no future in England's dreaming!" and shouted "We mean it, ma-a-an!"—as if there were any question. In "Anarchy in the U.K.," a Dolls-influenced anthem for annihilating the complacent, Rotten hollered, "I am an Antichrist! I am an anarchist! Don't know what I want but I know how to get it! I wanna destroy passers-by. 'Cos I wan-na be-ee-ee-ay an-ar-kaa-aa-ay!"

On November 6, 1975, the Sex Pistols—Rotten, Matlock, Jones, and Cook—played their first show at Matlock's school, the suburban St. Martin's College of Art. Two songs into their raw, Spartan set, the school's social programmer pulled the plug on them. A legend was born.

Contrary to popular myth, the Sex Pistols didn't emerge fully formed, without influences or antecedents. Early rehearsal tapes reveal cover versions of songs by Jonathan Richman ("Road Runner"), the Who ("Substitute"), and the Monkees ("Stepping Stone"). But they denied everything and everyone when they spoke. In later years, after he lightened up, Lydon talked about this. "I can point at things that used to impress me," he told J. D. Considine. "That would have been the New York Dolls, Iggy, Alice Cooper, T. Rex, Captain Beefheart, even Neil Young."

Some of the starting points are obvious, like the Dolls (Jones's guitar sound, not to mention the McLaren connection) and Captain Beefheart (the band's penchant for musical and personal disharmony). Neil Young, who Lydon saw on his landmark 1975 U.K. tour, is a more surprising choice, albeit an appropriate one. Although Young made his millions as a wan folk-rock heartthrob, what motivated him most effectively was edgy, barbed rock and roll that motored as far away as possible from convention.

His greatest album, *Tonight's The Night,* the record his 1975 tour supported, is one of rock and roll's most brutal works, an unflinching dissection of the desolation of heroin addiction. Young had recently lost two close associates to junk, and he was so close to his subject matter that he kept picking at it, like a festering sore, through the album, over and over, until it hurt so hard he had to scream. In this way, he's among the group's most direct antecedents.

In the months that followed their first, aborted performance, the Sex Pistols collected a fanatically devoted following that sported Sex shop anti-fashions and wild, spiked hair spray-painted the most outrageous colors—blue, green, or any bright combination—they could imagine. The fans were as violent as the ideas in Rotten's poison-pen lyrics, so many nights the band showed up at a gig only to find that wary promoters had canceled it. (A few times, the band advertised itself as the Spots, an acronym for Sex Pistols on Tour Secretly.) Although violence was always a possibility, many performances had their moments of unvarnished hilarity. At one show, Sex clerk Jordan introduced the Sex Pistols as "if possible, even better than the lovely Joni Mitchell."

Many shows were picketed. Said one protester to a TV camera, "I've got two teenage daughters. I don't mind if they go to see Rod Stewart, but not this rubbish." This, of course, was exactly McLaren's method: Polarize and infiltrate.

The impact on the crowd of the performances that did take place cannot be overestimated. Mike Peters was a seventeen-year-old Welsh kid who wanted to be in a rock band, but he felt so distanced from the music he heard on the radio that he didn't know where to start. One night, the Sex Pistols pointed him in the right direction.

"The attitude was incredible," Peters remembers. "Right in your face. They were singing words and ideas I'd never heard before. None of us had ever heard anyone say something like 'You're so pretty vacant.' We had nothing to compare it to. The Sex Pistols made us think about things we'd never thought about before. Their attitude was incredible. After the show, I was so taken aback by the energy that I walked up to the bar to try to talk to Johnny Rotten. I asked him, 'Where does it all come from? How can you write songs like "Pretty Vacant"?' And he just turned his back on me, turned away. It left me cold, but it also got me excited. The music had really hit me deep inside in a way I didn't understand at all. I felt ready to burst, and I just needed someone to talk to. But Johnny Rotten wouldn't talk to me, and I took that as his way of telling me I had to do it for myself. He wasn't going to do it for me. Even though the Sex Pistols went on to become a joke, I think that most of the people who saw them saw potential. The main impact of the Pistols was not their message but that people could almost see right through them and still find something there."

Frustration over the lack of steady work, frustration over the unending violence that emerged from the crowd, and frustration that Matlock's love for straightforward pop music was undermining Rotten's improvised nihilism, prompted Matlock's firing in early March 1977. He was replaced almost immediately by John Beverly Ritchie, a London thug and occasional Sex shop boy who was Rotten's only friend back in his school years. Partly out of affection for Rotten and partly because this burgeoning scene of violence attracted him, Ritchie was one of the Sex Pistols' most enthusiastic and most visible fans. He attended almost all their early gigs, and his wild up-and-down dancing (he accidentally invented the pogo) and uncontrollable outbursts were often as integral to the show as the band's music even before he joined the band. Because Ritchie's most visible pleasure came from attacking random people with a bicycle chain, Rotten bestowed upon him the title Sid Vicious. It stuck.

"They were really close mates," Glen Matlock told British journalists Julie Birchill and Tony Parsons after he had been sacked. "After John joined the band, Rotten didn't see so much of Vicious because now he had the Pistols. Vicious used to be ringing him up all the time and Rotten just used to take the piss out of Vicious, really put him down. I think that Sid felt a bit left out. And that's when he started beating people up."

Nobody ever claimed Sid could play bass, but McLaren knew this boy had the right attitude. Violence was always a possibility when he was around. Ask Nick Kent, the British music journalist and occasional McLaren confidant who wrote the wrong words about Sid and got stomped as a result. Vicious was unpredictable, and that was what McLaren believed the band needed: better a hooligan than a tunesmith.

The band was earning headlines, and the band members had to live up to the sensationalism that was expected of them.

By the time Matlock got the boot, McLaren and the Sex Pistols had already swindled (to steal a term from McLaren's textbook for impresarios) their first record company. In November 1976, barely a year after their first gig, EMI—the most prestigious label in England, the folks who gave us the Beatles—won a furious bidding war and paid an advance of £40,000 for the privilege of releasing the Sex Pistols' product. EMI was establishment but it smelled the money to be made off the punk fad.

Not that the band wasn't suspicious of EMI. When label representatives showed up unexpectedly at an early recording session, McLaren wrote EMI IS HERE in lipstick on the window separating the performance room from the control room. What more encouragement did the band members need to act up?

On November 26, 1976, EMI released the band's first single, a blistering take of "Anarchy in the U.K." and the uproar it caused was part of what got the band onto the high-rated Bill Grundy local talk show on ITV. (A last-minute cancellation by another band, allegedly Queen, didn't hurt, either.)

In two tense, hilarious minutes the evening of December 1, the band breathed more life into the talk-show format than anyone imagined possible. When Grundy asked how the £40,000 advance from EMI had been spent, he learned from Jones, "Well, we fuckin' spent it, ain't we? It's all gone, down the boozer." Communication broke down entirely during an exchange between Rotten and an increasingly exasperated Grundy, who for some reason was praising Beethoven, Mozart, Bach, and Brahms.

"They're wonderful people," Rotten said of his dubious antecedents, with the forced dramatics one expects in a put-on. "They really turn us on." Rotten bobbed back and forth approximating an Orthodox Jew lost in prayer—but it was really the effects of amphetamines.

Not sure what to make of this (everyone was in on the joke except for the interviewer), Grundy asked, in a bit of a non sequitur, "Well, suppose they turn someone else on?"

Mumbling, commenting more on Grundy than talking to him, Rotten let out, "That's their tough shit."

Grundy pushed the provocation as far as he could, asking Rotten to repeat "the rude word" and chatting up Siouxsie Sioux, one of the Sex Pistols' hangers-on who was hovering behind the band. The floodgates opened. Responding to Grundy's feigned pick-up of Sioux, in ten seconds Jones called Grundy a "dirty sod," a "dirty old man," a "dirty bastard," a "dirty fucker," and a "fucking rotter." Grundy called for an end to the show. While the credits rolled, the band members laughed at him, somewhere between pity and derision.

By the following morning's papers, the establishment attacked, in articles with headlines like FOUR-LETTER PUNK-ROCK GROUP IN TV STORM and SWEARING IS BANNED AT HOME, SAYS MRS. GRUNDY. More Sex Pistols shows were banned (Grundy himself was suspended for two weeks) and the band members made themselves even less welcome the first week of 1977 when they vomited in public at Heathrow Airport before they boarded a KLM flight to Amsterdam.

A month after the Grundy appearance, EMI had had enough. The company paid the band another £50,000 to get them off their clean-minded, clean-mouthed label, and on January 6, EMI issued a statement that read: "EMI and the Sex Pistols have mutually agreed to terminate their recording agreement. EMI feels it is unable to promote this group's records internationally in view of the adverse publicity which has been generated over the last two months, although recent press reports of the behavior of the Sex Pistols appear to have been exaggerated. The termination of the contract with the Sex Pistols does not in any way affect EMI's intention to remain active in all areas of the music business." EMI's statement made clear that although the company was still anxious to make money off punk, it didn't want to deal with the ramifications of such an association.

McLaren slipped into a brief depression—the departure from the country's most prestigious label was anything but a mutual decision—but he was up and scheming within a week. On March 9, 1977, McLaren and the Sex Pistols set out on their second record-company swindle. Executives at A&M Records staged a contract signing for an advance for £150,000 in front of Buckingham Palace (a perfect received-by-McLaren juxtaposition). The band members traveled to A&M's corporate offices and allegedly spit wine on the carpet, shit out windows, and had sex with secretaries. (They denied it all and no charges were ever pressed.)

Within the next three days, Rotten was fined £40 for a previous amphetamine-possession conviction, and the rest of the band attacked "hip" London disk jockey Bob Harris and his sound engineer, leaving the latter with cuts that took fourteen stitches to close. They decided that the cover art for the first A&M single, "God Save the Queen," was to be a graphic, by McLaren's art college friend Jamie Reid, with Elizabeth II blindfolded, a safety pin through her nose. The sleeve was the perfect antidote to the Silver Jubilee, the twenty-fifth anniversary of Elizabeth's ascension to the British throne.

A&M officials, prodded by such performers on their label as Karen Carpenter, Peter Frampton, Supertramp, and Rick Wakeman, decided that capitalizing on a fad was all well and good, but that the Sex Pistols were too hot—and too ugly—to handle. One day McLaren visited A&M managing director Derek Green and read upside down on his host's desk a Telex from keyboard wizard Wakeman, a friend of Green's, asking if he now had to get a safety pin through his nose so he could stay on the label. McLaren broadcast this to the press (although he acted as if he missed the point that Wakeman's Telex from Montreux was a joke).

Ten days after A&M signed the Sex Pistols, the company destroyed the 25,000 copies of "God Save the Queen" it had pressed and paid the Sex Pistols £75,000 to leave its offices and never come back. The Sex Pistols were the most famous band in England, and they had no records for sale. When Virgin Records finally signed them on May 13, 1977, and released the rabid, ironic "God Save the Queen," the record sold two million copies although it had been blacklisted by the official TV and radio stations and chain stores. It was a massive, unprecedented, totally underground smash hit.

Virgin was a smaller, iconoclastic label best known for its epic Mike Oldfield hit "Tubular Bells," which became the theme for *The Exorcist*. Its then-current advertisement for *Green*, an album by Steve Hillage, depicts the album cover and reads: "Inside this sleeve you will not find, tedious hippy music, half-baked philosophy, late-sixties metaphysics, or unkind thoughts. Inside this sleeve you will find laser-intensive guitar playing and innovating [sic] rock and roll music. Listen to it and find out." Few bothered.

At this point, the anarchy Rotten had prophesied came back at him with full force. Although most Sex Pistols shows had to be promoted primarily through word of mouth (few legitimate papers would print advertisements for them), the band members were visible figures—and easy targets. In June, Rotten's leg was slashed in a parking lot; a week later two toughs smashed his face with a broken glass and reopened the cut in his leg. The same week, drummer Paul Cook was accosted in the Shepherd's Bush tube station by six men who used iron bars to split his head open. Fifteen stitches sealed it.

Through all this, McLaren stood back, watched, smiled, counted the money, and managed it indifferently. He continued to scheme—he tried to make a Sex Pistols movie with American skin-film director Russ Meyer and young screenwriter Roger Ebert—but he mostly sat back and watched.

The aborted film *Who Killed Bambi?* was McLaren's first significant experience with American collaborators as the Sex Pistols' manager. It shows how much of a stretch it was for him to translate his provincial ideas about the band into an international phenomenon.

McLaren and the Sex Pistols knew about Meyer and Ebert because their rock-parody film *Beyond the Valley of the Dolls* was a cult success in London, along the lines of *The Rocky Horror Picture Show.* They were attracted to Meyer because he had a reputation as an iconoclast, and McLaren was able to convince 20th Century Fox in London to at least consider financing the film. McLaren told Meyer and Ebert that the money was already in the bank.

"McLaren had some kind of production deal put together in his mind if not on paper," says Ebert. "I flew to Los Angeles and I moved into the Sunset Marquis Hotel with a typewriter and a card table and started writing the screenplay, in cooperation with Russ and to a lesser degree Malcolm, who I remember wore bondage pants. McLaren struck me as a bright guy with an irreverent sense of humor. Many managers talk about groups with a sense of devotion and awe, but he didn't take the Sex Pistols seriously. Russ and I were quite free to construct an absurd screenplay."

The film, briefly titled *Anarchy in the U.K.* before the parties settled on *Who Killed Bambi?*, has nothing to do with *The Great Rock and Roll Swindle*, the later, incoherent Sex Pistols film directed (if you can call it that) by Julian Temple. For *Who Killed Bambi?*, Ebert wrote a story in which the Pistols try to overthrow the rock establishment, with the lead villain named M.J., an obvious euphemism for Mick Jagger. Marianne Faithfull was to play Sid's mother; they were going to shoot up together and have a violent, incestuous relationship. "All this was suggested by Malcolm," says Ebert. "The Pistols had no input at all. The script was done and approved in three weeks."

Ebert's script climaxed with M.J., after revitalizing his career by impersonating Rotten, being killed as the Sex Pistols crashed the party celebrating his comeback. The script's final words belonged to Rotten:

"Will success spoil Johnny? No! He will waste, spoil, smash, blow up, and destroy success!" After Rotten kicked M.J.'s dead body, Ebert had Rotten stare at the camera and, in a voice just above a whisper, ask, "Did ya ever have the feeling yer bein' watched?" It was an ending out of the dreams of punks. The Sex Pistols take over the pop-music world and refuse to succumb to its trappings.

Ebert joined Meyer in London in August to do rewrites for a week with the Sex Pistols. "Johnny related with Russ," Ebert says. "Russ treated him like a punk. Russ is a tall, strapping World War II veteran who climbs mountains. Russ told Johnny things like, 'Listen, you little punk, we fought the Battle of Britain for you.' We got along pretty well. Sid was a great deal more distant. He was hostile and withdrawn."

Meyer and Ebert knew McLaren was having cash-flow problems (the Fox money was becoming less likely, and he went through the record company advances quickly; anarchy in the free market doesn't come cheap), but they stuck around because McLaren was about to nail down a sizable American record deal, most likely with Warner Brothers. Still, Meyer had to be paid at the beginning of a week if McLaren expected him to work that week. Meyer simply didn't believe Malcolm had any money.

"Russ felt that the only hope for the film was if Malcolm gave him total production control," Ebert says. "Russ had experience. Malcolm was more concerned with being producer in his own mind. Russ built sets, and shot for a day and a half. The electricians and technicians refused to work until they were paid by Malcolm. They weren't, so production shut down."

As the film unraveled, the band wrapped up its debut LP for Virgin, *Never Mind the Bollocks, Here's the Sex Pistols* ("bollocks" is British slang for "balls"), recorded with producer Chris Thomas. (Early recording efforts with session guitarist Chris Spedding and band sound man Dave Goodman were failures, although Goodman kept the master tapes and later sold them.) McLaren mostly concerned himself with more ways to exploit the group and its would-be exploiters. He brought the band to the Continent, where they encountered more violence offstage and on: Sid Vicious could create a commotion almost by instinct.

It was around this time that Vicious, who had just been introduced to heroin by American girlfriend/groupie/junkie Nancy Spungen, started to direct his brutality inward. His arms were full of needle marks and cigarette burns, and his chest, frequently bare in concert, revealed razor and knife slashes. McLaren had started to fear Vicious—Spungen encouraged and extended the existing rift between them—but realized that Vicious was his meal ticket. One attempt by McLaren and his office manager Sophie Richmond to kidnap Spungen—under the guise of bringing her to the dentist—and forcibly deport her to the U.S., backfired badly.

If Johnny Rotten was the voice of punk, Sid Vicious was the look. Live fast, die young, leave a good-looking corpse if you're lucky: McLaren saw Sid as the James Dean of punk even if Sid's viciousness was far less studied than anyone imagined. McLaren was certain Vicious would die on him, but until then he was going to exploit him. McLaren saw himself as the Colonel Tom Parker of the Sex Pistols. And like Parker, he schemed to conquer the biggest prize of all: America.

Like all great rock and roll, going back to Elvis Presley and Jerry Lee Lewis at Sun Records, the Sex Pistols upset the establishment. The Beatles, the Rolling Stones, and the Who did the same in the early- and mid-sixties, but the Sex Pistols offer up far uglier visions than any of their predecessors. After all, it's an uglier time. Elvis isn't young and screaming "Hound Dog" anymore. He's dead, a sad lesson to young rockers.

It's ugly in the Sex Pistols' England. When Margaret Thatcher and the Tories took power and started disassembling the welfare state, among the first to notice they'd been hit were young, male, and poor. This was the group that made up the Sex Pistols' membership, as well as their audience. When the Sex Pistols play a song that damns the country's beloved monarch ("God save the Queen/A fascist regime/She made you a moron"), they give a voice to the anger and the aspirations of their audience. The privileged pop stars aren't even bothering to address such issues anymore.

It's ugly in America, too. The Carter administration is about to go under thanks to the disenchantment double-digit inflation and unemployment bring. With the execution of Gary Gilmore, capital punishment is back for the first time in a decade. David Berkowitz, the "Son of Sam" murderer, is terrorizing New York. Violence is back. People are becoming polarized (a situation that Ronald Reagan will exploit to defeat Carter) and anesthetized. This malaise informs the day's hit music. American pop is split into several competing fronts. If you want to dance all over your troubles, you can put on your shiny leisure suit, head down to the disco, and strut to Donna Summer's latest. If you want to hear self-confident young men babble on about how important they are to the world, you can save up twelve dollars and head down to the local arena to see Styx or Queen or the Eagles. If you want to feel smart and sensitive, you can cuddle up at home with a James Taylor record.

None of these subgenres have anything to do with provoking action. Disco divas want their listeners to surrender to the beat, arena-rock boys want their listeners to surrender themselves to the overblown ideas in the songs, and the singer/songwriters want their listeners to retreat within and rediscover themselves. In all cases, the music serves to keep the listener and performer far apart. No common ground is broken, nothing is exchanged, nothing is demanded, nothing is delivered.

With few exceptions, rock and roll in 1977 comes down to reinforcing barriers that already exist and putting up some new ones. The Sex Pistols are doing the opposite. They are the voice of the crowd, the people who are being shunned by the rest. They are breaking down the barriers, and erecting in their place something refreshing in its overt, magnificent ugliness.

There is punk-influenced music in America coming from such performers as Talking Heads and poet-turned-singer Patti Smith and her Group, but those bands are too cerebral, tentative, and mannered to shock anyone. New York's Ramones, the band that started it all and the one dangerous unit among them, seem content to appear as cartoon-character goons. (When the Sex Pistols went in to record their first single, the band showed up at the studio with a copy of the Ramones' first record. That is what they wanted to sound like.) These bands are all hovering under the surface; they need a vile, angry group to lead them over the top—and that's where the Sex Pistols fit in.

The Sex Pistols come to America at a crucial time for rock-and-roll music and pop culture at large. Rock has splintered into competing camps. The singular rock community of the late sixties, the one encouraged by violent events to rebel and make Woodstock and Monterey, the one that helped end a war and broaden the everyday rights of many groups, is long gone. Some fans listen to disco from Donna Summer and *Saturday Night Fever,* some opt for insular singer-songwriter music from James Taylor and Paul Simon, some prefer sweet Los Angeles pop from the Eagles and Linda Ronstadt, some enjoy the faceless midwestern supergroups Styx and R.E.O. Speedwagon.

Major figures in all those movements date their performance debuts back to the sixties: they're old-timers and their strongest work is behind them. If they talk directly to the kids in the crowd, it's only because they haven't matured themselves.

A name like the Sex Pistols is eerily, subversively appropriate There's some danger in it, a hint of S&M, but with party-all-the-time the existing aesthetic, a band with Sex in their name makes sense. The irony, of course, is that like the shop Sex, the Sex Pistols have nothing to do with sex. They are four ugly, scary people. But their name has gotten them some attention; McLaren's calculated infiltration can begin.

The America that the Sex Pistols are coming to in the late seventies is one in which the message of many of the rock stars is "If you have money, come on in and spend it on us; if not, stay far away." You need the toys to join this club. The Ramones, Patti Smith Group, and Talking Heads have had to make a music of their own, a music that reflects their own fears, longings, and hopes. They appeal mostly to the cognoscenti, but they are getting across at least to some of those who can't stomach what they hear on the radio. Rock has always appealed to rebels, teenagers, those who feel left out. When the Ramones sing their signature tune "Sheena Is a Punk Rocker," they're celebrating. Sheena has alienated her friends by denying the disco life and is now a punk. She is different and proud of it; she is the perfect heroine for the movement.

CHAPTER TWO
Setting the Stage

IT'S NOVEMBER 1977. *Saturday Night Fever* and the allure of white, tailor-made leisure suits rule, but four bad boys from London are forcing a substantial undercurrent. The Sex Pistols have polarized everyone who has heard them in England and Europe. It's time for Americans to choose sides. Warner Brothers has signed them and is preparing to release a domestic version of *Never Mind the Bollocks, Here's the Sex Pistols.* Bob Regehr, the man who signed the Sex Pistols to Warner Brothers, has committed a large promotional budget to breaking the band in particular and "New Wave" in general in America.

(Major labels use "New Wave" as a euphemism for punk rock in an attempt to make bands like the Sex Pistols sound more palatable to the mainstream. A late 1977 issue of "Bunny Droppings," a newsletter sent out by the Warner Brothers publicity department, refers to the signing of "those notorious musical anarchists" and states that the signing places the company "firmly in the forefront of the New Wave." You can almost hear them pat their own backs.)

Regehr is an anomaly, a vice-president for a major American label who lives more for music than money, although he's able to satisfy the corporate heads by finding strong performers who can keep the company in the black. Even one of his most decidedly noncommercial performers, Randy Newman, has just released "Short People," which is on its way to becoming an unlikely Number Two smash. Regehr takes chances. That makes the Sex Pistols an ideal group for him.

It also makes him the ideal conduit for the Sex Pistols, as far as McLaren and Rory Johnston, McLaren's American representative and the point man on the U.S. record deals, are concerned. MCA and Arista make offers for the band, and meet indifference. Casablanca comes in at the last minute and tops the Warner Brothers offer but they're too late: The band is set on Warners.

"They're a hip label," Johnston tells McLaren. "They have Captain Beefheart, they have Bob Regehr." Sources close to the company maintain that the long-term record and movie deal the band signs with Warner Brothers carries an advance tag of roughly $700,000.

It's in Warner Brothers' interest to break both the Sex Pistols and "New Wave": The conglomerate also distributes Sire Records, the home of the Ramones and Talking Heads.

Carl Scott, director of artist relations, reports to Regehr. "He dreamt it, and I enforced it," he says. "Signing the Sex Pistols was crazy and great. They were a bizarre band with a terrific, difficult reputation. I didn't understand the music at all, but Regehr understood it completely. They were factions within Warner Brothers who couldn't figure out why we'd want to do it, but Regehr felt very passionate about it. He felt it was the future in some way."

The signing of the Sex Pistols upsets a large group of Warner Brothers employees. "We had lots of apprehensions about the Pistols at Warner Brothers," says Bob Merlis, the label's director of publicity. "A lot of people in the company thought that Regehr's signing them was a crackpot idea. They were an avowedly unmusical entity, and we weren't used to that. I was dubious at first. I thought we were buying ourselves lots of trouble. Then I realized we were part of one of the greatest events in rock-and-roll history. It was the coolest move we could possibly have made. It made Warner Brothers seem that much more with it than any other label, especially EMI and A&M. We had the guts to sign them while everyone else was running away. I thought if we can make money while they kick our ass, we get the last laugh. I know I sound kind of McLarenesque here."

The rock industry at large doesn't understand, either. A headline in the December 4 Green Bay *Press-Gazette* says it all: MOST PUNK RHYMES WITH JUNK. If that's not enough, try this lead in the December 1 Rice *Thrasher:* THIS ALBUM SUCKS! THIS ALBUM SUCKS! THIS ALBUM SUCKS!

Most Warner Brothers people steer clear. Says Scott, "I didn't want any kind of relationship with the band. I stayed at a distance. I was afraid of them. Sid was someone who would carve his chest open. He's not the kind of guy you want to take to lunch."

Internal dissension notwithstanding, Regehr commits to McLaren to underwrite a major U.S. tour. Most of Regehr's day-to-day dealings with McLaren go through Johnston, a Brit based in southern California who'd met the band in 1975, when he was going to art school days and working nights as a barman in the Portobello, a London hotel the band frequented.

"I knew Malcolm and I knew what he was trying to do in the States," Johnston says. "I knew the philosophy behind the band. I felt I could do something with them in the States. I knew the techniques Malcolm had used, without realizing that they would have to be adapted for America. The time was ripe in England for the political message. In America, the message was going to translate on a more musical level."

Regehr wants to put out the American version of *Never Mind the Bollocks, Here's the Sex Pistols* as quickly as possible, partly because he has competition. Richard Branson, the head of Virgin Records, has managed to get the master tapes of the album considerably in advance of Warner Brothers. The official release date of the Virgin LP is October 28, but copies appear in stores two full weeks before the release date (which was supposed to be simultaneous with the American version). The British LP is in import shops before the jacket copy for the U.S. version is finalized. The import is selling briskly, taking tens of thousands of potential sales away from Warner Brothers. Warner Brothers finally releases its version of the LP on November 11, but it takes another week to get it into most stores. Partially as a response to the lost sales that result from a month of unchallenged parallel imports, Johnston feels the pressure from Warner Brothers to undertake a comprehensive tour as soon as possible.

Meanwhile in England, the title *Never Mind the Bollocks* hasn't gotten by the Nottingham police without a fight. Julia Story, a police sergeant, found the title obscene and hauled in all the shopkeepers she could find who stocked the record. After a brief, pointless obscenity trial (the charges were brought under the century-old, Victorian-era Indecent Advertisement Act), the word is allowed.

"It's great!" Rotten tells the waiting press when he leaves the courtroom. "Bollocks is legal! Bollocks! Bollocks! Bollocks!"

In New York, Barbara Skydel, from the respected booking agency Premier Talent, the company whose founder, Frank Barsalona, virtually invented big-time rock tours in the mid-sixties, prepares to book the Sex Pistols' American tour, along with Johnston and Monk.

Everyone at Warner Brothers has heard the horror stories about the band's alleged antics; nobody wants to deal with them. It's a high-priority project, but it's avoided by the bigwigs. They want to make money off the band, but they don't want to be in the same room with them.

Monk has worked as a tour manager frequently over the past decade for most major companies, more and more frequently for Warner Brothers. He has just gotten off the road as a tour manager for Chunky, Novi, and Ernie (a soul-influenced lounge act that time has graciously forgotten) and is down in the Caribbean recovering from the experience.

Monk calls Carl Scott and asks if there is anything happening at Warner Brothers, anything he could work on. He doesn't tell Scott that he's almost broke.

"Regehr's just signed the Sex Pistols," Scott says.

"Yeah, I heard. What are they like?"

"I'd rather not find out. We can't find anyone in America who we think can work with them. No one good'll touch them. You've heard the wild stories. You've gotten addicts to do professional tours. You could handle it, couldn't you?"

Monk jumps at it. "When do I fly up?"

Monk arrives in New York in mid-November. He is hired at five hundred dollars a week to do promotion, artist development, and production/tour managing, including logistics. He commandeers an office at Warner Brothers and plays the record over and over.

Regehr advocates a nationwide tour and flies Johnston first class to New York to meet with Skydel and Barsalona. Johnston tries to check in at the Waldorf-Astoria, where Regehr has reserved him a room. But Johnston's normal street clothes—basic black, just a shade tamer than punk attire—see to it that the hotel personnel won't let him register. The next day, an executive from Warner Brothers has to come over and convince the Waldorf staff that Johnston indeed belongs there.

"The whole trip was quite novel," says Johnston. "Here I was, being escorted around New York, being courted by everyone under the sun. After my first meeting with Barbara, she took me out to dinner with Sid Bernstein, the guy who did the Beatles at Shea Stadium. The stories he told me! How he organized the Beatles' Shea Stadium concert on the fly, with no organization, just a post office box at Grand Central Station. I was made to feel that I was being made privy to that interesting, inside kind of life."

Skydel continues pressing for a professional tour, without much help from McLaren. McLaren's conception of an American tour is far different from the Premier status quo. At first he wants the Sex Pistols to do only three dates: the Apollo Theater in New York; Tupelo, Mississippi (because it is the birthplace of Elvis Presley); and Tijuana. After Regehr and Skydel talk him out of it, he makes his second offer: a comprehensive, full-fledged tour—of Texas. McLaren has a vision of a Texas full of rednecks waiting to be outraged by the Sex Pistols. McLaren had toured part of the South back in his days as a crutch for the New York Dolls; he likes the idea of staying relatively underground and keeping away from the country's premier media centers.

"Malcolm had this misguided notion that the South was all poor," says Skydel. "He thought that's who the Sex Pistols' fans would be. He didn't know America, and he had cockeyed notions about it. He didn't know there would be rednecks who'd want to kill the band. It wasn't that calculating. He didn't realize."

A Texas-only tour is unacceptable to the Americans, and Regehr, Skydel, and Johnston forge a compromise. The Sex Pistols will play the southern venues McLaren so dearly wants—but not until after they play the North. Going against his boss, Johnston pushes for the northern dates, feeling that shows in blue-collar industrial cities like Cleveland, Pittsburgh, and Cincinnati would keep to McLaren's concept of "bringing the music to the real people."

McLaren refuses to play New York (Regehr tosses out the idea of playing Madison Square Garden for one dollar a seat), but allows a San Francisco date. "Great," McLaren says. "We'll tear down San Francisco. We'll ram it up the hippies' asses." Finally, McLaren gives in on playing New York after the Sex Pistols are offered a spot on *Saturday Night Live*. After that performance, the first leg of the tour will take the band across the northern half of the country in late December and early January in the South through January. The early dates are December 30 at the Leona Theater, Homestead, Pennsylvania; December 31 at the Ivanhoe Theatre, Chicago; January 1 at the Agora Theatre, Cleveland; and January 3 at the Alexandria Rolling Rink, in Alexandria, Virginia. Then they'll drive south to Atlanta and start the tour McLaren wants most. At Johnston's request, Skydel signs the Ohio band Pere Ubu to open most of the northern dates.

McLaren insists that ticket prices be kept low. The Sex Pistols aren't playing large halls because the band can't fill them yet, but they aren't even playing places where they would be expected to have an audience. They're avoiding the major markets by design: There are more punks in New York than anywhere else, but McLaren refuses to let the band put on a full show there. He's a punk Tom Parker, a carny who wants to play all the sideshows.

McLaren demands a ticket price of two dollars. The promoters cry foul, so Premier raises the price to three-fifty per ticket, still incredibly low (arena-concert ticket prices average eleven-fifty). "The tour is for the working class," McLaren informs Skydel. "The prices must reflect that. Besides, I'm sure Warner Brothers will be happy to part with the rest."

Bob Merlis joins in on the fun and gets with Regehr's program. He proposes not to give away any tickets to the press, since the tickets are so cheap. "We'll sell them to show continuity with McLaren's concept of revolution to the people," he enthuses. Regehr loves the idea, as does the band.

To keep the promoters happy in the midst of this (the label is going to take a bath on this, the promoters think, but we're not), Warner Brothers agrees to cover the inevitable shortfalls the promoters will confront. (See document page 37.)

Monk and the crew await the band's arrival. The tour is to start December 30 in Pittsburgh.

The band is supposed to come into the country around Christmas. By that time Monk has assembled the road crew, the equipment, the trucks, the bodyguards. He normally doesn't hit the road with a new band from England with a full security force. That's usually reserved for tours with more popular bands like the Rolling Stones. But he knows that this will be different. Promoters are worried about riots. There is more than a smidgen of hysteria on everyone's part. Monk tries to treat this like a normal tour, but everybody knows it isn't.

On December 29, on the way to their flight at Heathrow Airport, the band members are denied American visas. Embassy officials cite "excludable" offenses; Warner Brothers sends immigration-law whiz Ted Jaffe, who previously got the Rolling Stones into the U.S. when their visas had been denied, to solve the matter. (The company also instructs its spokespeople to use Jaffe's respected name "often and whenever possible.")

All is soon sorted out, but one thing is apparent. Intentionally or not, McLaren has doomed the northern half of the tour. Only the southern dates, starting January 5 in Atlanta, can be salvaged. Perhaps the northern dates can be rescheduled later. McLaren's marketing strategy dictates that he doesn't want his band to play in the North, and now they're not going to. He perceives there will be trouble down south; that's where the headlines will be and that's where he wants the band. McLaren doesn't even apply for visas until a day before the projected Pittsburgh show, although he knows the band members all have criminal records

PREMIER TALENT AGENCY   THREE EAST 54TH ST., NEW YORK, N.Y. 10022 · TELEPHONE (212) 758-4900

December 27, 1977

Mr. Noel Monk
Warner Bros. Records
3 East 54th Street
New York, New York 10022

Dear Noel:

Per your instructions, we have advised Sam L'Hommadieu that he
is going to receive a $1,000 production fee for promoting the
Sex Pistols date in Alexandria, Virginia, and that Warner
Bros. will make up the difference between the potential gross
and the actual costs which at this point is an estimate of
$858, if the date sells out.

Also, we have a call in to Bill Graham advising him that he
will receive a $500 fee from Warner Bros. for promoting the
San Francisco date, and that the difference between the
potential gross of $4,000 and the projected cost of the show
(including talent) of $8,090 will also be paid for by Warner
Bros.

                              Regards,

                              Barbara Skydel
                              Executive Vice/President

BS:mm
cc: Bob Regehr
     Rory Johnston
     Carl Scott

that will take time to explain away, even with a Ted Jaffe on retainer.

When he hears that the band's visas have been denied, Monk draws the short straw and calls the promoters of the canceled dates. The promoter of the Ivanhoe (in Chicago) cries. Yet if the promoters are in tears over the cancellations, Warner Brothers' Ted Cohen should be in hysterics.

Cohen's role on the tour is a challenging one, far more difficult than his usual assignments. After two weeks with the Sex Pistols, he'll be on the road with teenybopper pin-up Shaun Cassidy. As the company's national director for special projects, Cohen's role here is to get as much radio and retail-store awareness of the Sex Pistols. The only catch is that he has to succeed without any help from the band members. The Sex Pistols do not stoop to radio promotions, McLaren informs him. Cohen knows the band is not going to get much radio play even if Sid and Johnny move into the control rooms, but he still has to get radio and retail excited.

In Pittsburgh, he succeeds. He meets with officials from National Record Mart, a major retailer, and convinces them that the Sex Pistols' show in town will be an event, that the focus of the rock world will be on Pittsburgh. He further convinces them to let him fill all their window displays with album covers, posters, and T-shirts that all warn, WATCH THIS SPACE. They plan to do that for seven days, and on the eighth day they will switch the display to the Sex Pistols, announcing the availability of the record and the tour date.

Five days into this plan, the northern dates are canceled. National Record Mart is furious with Warner Brothers. This was the week before Christmas, not a great time to have one's display windows essentially empty. They wonder if the label is playing a joke on them.

Yet the evidence strongly suggests that it is McLaren who played a joke on Warner Brothers and Premier. Johnston says McLaren's rationale in avoiding New York was more than polemical. He was worried about Sid. "Malcolm wanted to stop Sid from getting completely out of control. Sid was with Nancy Spungen, and she was talking him up on how great New York was and how much smack they'd get there. He was in the early stages of being strung out, and I think

Malcolm knew from his experience with the New York Dolls that if he put Sid in New York there would be trouble. There would be too many druggie people who knew who Sid was, and he'd know who they were. He was going to hook up with them and disappear into the night, and we'd never see him again. In London, Malcolm had made attempts several times to get Sid some doctor's help. Malcolm had made attempts to deal with Sid, but not in a crisis fashion. The problem was getting Sid to want to kick junk. And Sid didn't want to kick junk."

Johnston shifts some of the blame from McLaren to Vicious. "Sid believed his own press. He was the ultimate rock and roller in that way. He couldn't play a note of music, but he was an incredible character. He was the personification of the ultimate fan even before Malcolm got to him. Perhaps Malcolm should have thought not to put this kid in this situation because he's going to go completely over the top. But he was over the top before Malcolm put him in the band. Sid wasn't something Malcolm had created."

The fortitude of Warner Brothers also surprises McLaren. Johnston adds, "I don't think Malcolm realized how committed Warner Brothers was going to be to getting the band their visas. They made a lot of waves in Washington. There were convictions against these guys—more than we realized. We knew Johnny had a minor drug offense, one of those accidental things where he had a tiny amount of speed. Jones had a burglary conviction. Paul had gotten into trouble, and Sid had beaten up a cop. The one that was most innocuous was the drug conviction, but that was the hardest one to waive. Malcolm was surprised that Warners got off their ass and really did something about it and got them to America so quickly. The *Saturday Night Live* show was originally the cornerstone the tour was going to be built on. Then the visa thing happened, and that fell out. Malcolm should at least have let me know that he didn't want that show to happen."

Yet at the same time this imbroglio is proceeding, Johnston tells the American press that the band is skipping the show because they've decided to play for "their loyal English fans at home."

In the Sex Pistols' place, *Saturday Night Live* books Elvis

Costello and the Attractions, a punk-pigeonholed unit with major-label backing. Costello's drummer, Pete Thomas, wears a T-shirt that reads, THANX MALC. In the middle of playing a familiar song from his record, Costello orders the Attractions to stop the song dead. Lorne Michaels, the show's director, is terrified by the breach in decorum, and the network censor screams "Cut him off!" The sound consultant gambles on Costello, and the audience wins when Costello spirals into the scathing "Radio Radio," a damnation of American radio (of which NBC, the network that broadcasts *Saturday Night Live,* is a major part) that helps insure his longtime blackballing from it. It's a performance McLaren would have been proud of. It's a performance that could have been his.

Finally, on January 3, 1978, the band flies into New York. There are sixty photographers and press people waiting for them outside customs at JFK.

A reporter for the local all-news radio station WCBS-AM doesn't have any Sex Pistols to interview, so she confers with Monk. "We're trying to avoid any conversations with the press," he says.

"Don't worry about that from me," she responds. "Believe me, I don't want to meet them."

Most of the assembled are from the American press, but a few of their British colleagues have beaten the Sex Pistols to the States and are going to capture their first steps here. One of the paparazzi, tired of waiting, has become unruly.

"Could you please move back and give the band some space when they get off the plane?" Monk asks the photographer from the New York *Daily News.*

"Fuck you," the photographer spits back. "I'll go where I fucking want."

"Whatever you say, pal," Monk retorts and walks away. He returns with a dozen Port Authority policemen to help keep the photographers as far away from the band as Monk thinks is necessary.

Shit, Monk thinks, the band hasn't even touched down yet and already there's trouble. He hasn't seen anything yet.

TO _____   FROM: Alan Rosenberg _____

SUBJECT: _____

DATE: December 28, 1977 _____   COPIES TO: _____

C O N F I D E N T I A L

pending Violation

Sex Pistols: Arrest and Conviction Record

Sid Vicious (Legal name is John Simon Richie. The following were
           under the name of John Beverley Richie, mother's
           maiden name.)

B

1. May 27, 1974 - North London, Magistrate's Court
                   Assaulted two police officers.
    Disposition: discharged.
                  £5 ✻ cost for each policeman =£10 ✻   *assault a*

.   Same date, same court: Criminal damage.
    Disposition: £5 ✻   *settle as leave*
                          alone

2. Clerkenwell Magistrate's Court
    August 17, 1976 - Attempted taking and driving away
                      £20 ✻ fine and disqualified from driving
                      six months.
    Criminal damage: £10 ✻ plus £4 ✻ Court costs.

3. Wellestreet magistrate's court
    July 26, 1977 - Assault on police officer
    Result: £50 ✻ fine plus £25 ✻ costs   *wasn't arre Drug pending*

    Same cour-t, same date: Offensive weapon £10 ✻ fine.

John Lydon, aka Johnny Rotten

March 11, 1977 - Marlboro Street Magistrates Court
                 Possession of control drug Class "B" Amphetymine sulfate
                 under Section 5: Misuse of Drugs Act
                 £20 ✻ fine.

Paul Cook

1. Early 1975 (He doesn't remember exact date)
    Acton Magistrates Court - Theft £60 ✻ fine.

2. West London's Magistrate Court
    Mid-1975 - Thaft
    Result: Probation

Steve Jones

January 1976
All I have on him is theft,—£30 ✱ fine. Richmond Court.

INTER-OFFICE MEMO

WARNER BROS. RECORDS INC.

TO: The department   FROM: Merlis

SUBJECT: Sex Pistols birthdates

DATE: 10/28/77   COPIES TO: Liz, Les, Gary, Marion, Donna, Stacy, Pam, Heidi, Veron ica, Melenie, Suze, Nancy, Kathy

Following are the birthdates of the Sex Pistols.

Keep them on file somewhere (Sex Pistols clipping or bio file would be approiate, don't you thing) as people are starting to ask us these strange questions.

Johnny Rotten: Jan. 31, 1956

Steve Jones: Sept. 3, 1955

Paul Cook: July 20, 1956

Sid Viscious: May 10, 1957

I hope none of you try to figure out what signs these geezers were born under because, take it from me, they wuz all born under a bad sign.

CHAPTER THREE
Day One: Tuesday, January 3—New York to Atlanta

7 P.M.

FLIGHT #1 FROM LONDON, carrying the Sex Pistols, has just arrived at JFK's Pan Am International Terminal. Monk and his staff work to get the band through customs and out of the terminal as quickly as possible, but also in wait are sixty jostling reporters and photographers, all of whom are anxious to get the first shot of and interview with the Sex Pistols in America.

Monk has called Port Authority policemen to keep the assorted media, everyone from *The New York Times* to *High Times*, away from the band, with good reason. Back in England and Europe, band interviews, photo sessions, and promotional parties often deteriorated into violence, drugs, and, less frequently, sex (usually instigated by the photographers to get a more provocative image); the last thing the jet-lagged Sex Pistols want to see when they set foot in America is a hostile blaze of flash bulbs. Welcome.

Although he is outgunned by the press, Monk has his own weapons, legal weapons. Wary about what kind of problems the Sex Pistols will meet or cause on their American tour, Monk has outfitted members of the crew with Polaroid cameras and Norelco microcassette recorders. If anyone from the outside tries to instigate anything, they'll have all the evidence they need to escape liability (and the presence of cameras and tape recorders might help prevent problems in the first place). Monk has also arranged for the ultimate weapon for the crew and security guards: walkie-talkies (equipment that will soon become standard on many rock tours).

Still, all are leaning their cameras and microphones forward, contained but ready to shoot. Three hundred passengers from Flight #1, none of them likely to be confused for a punk rocker, file by. And then quiet.

After an uneasy minute, the door from customs bursts open, and the photographers all click their shutters and flash their bulbs at once. The lights temporarily blind the small group walking out the door, but they accept it and are pleasantly surprised. The only problem is that no one in the group has anything to do with the Sex Pistols. The focus of all the attention is a high-ranking official of the Greek Orthodox church and his attendants. The official is draped in flowing black robes and an ecclesiastical hat; he carries a scepter in his left hand. They walk by sheepishly, disappointed when they learn that none of the photographers or reporters consider them celebrities.

It's a pity McLaren isn't here with "my boys," the Sex Pistols. He'd love it. He'd walk slowly toward the photographers, absorbing the energy and gaining strength from them, while the band members, all visibly disoriented, follow him.

But McLaren isn't here. He's back in London, trying in vain to convince Russ Meyer that *Who Killed Bambi?* is a project worth resuscitating.

Instead, the customs door flies open again, revealing Steve Jones and Paul Cook wearing big, dopey grins—Bloody hell, this is America!—but the band's two front men are responding to the photographers just as Monk feared.

As Johnny Rotten walks by the photographers in his ratty green-plaid jacket and tangled pink tie, he stares with hate. He's a punk-rock Greta Garbo. He wants to be alone. He also wants them to look hard at him, so he can stare back even harder.

Sid Vicious, wearing grimy black jeans and a green T-shirt with a photograph of her royal majesty (a safety pin slashed through her face), greets the cameras with a raised middle finger and a sneer. His spiky black hair is a forest of Vaseline and talcum powder.

The image of Vicious's T-shirt comes from the queen-with-safety-pin picture sleeve to "God Save the Queen," and it encapsulates the Sex Pistols' attitude. Attack all that is sacred. The royal family sits pretty and gets fat in their palaces while the Sex Pistols and their audience queue on unemployment lines. All right, Sid doesn't actually say any of this, but you can extrapolate the raw idea from his ripped T-shirt even if he can't.

Monk tries to keep any ugliness out of the Pan Am terminal. He quickly introduces the security guards to the band members, none of whom seems willing to pay him any attention (let alone respect), and points them toward a tour bus waiting outside the terminal. As the band walks toward the bus, the photographers follow closely.

Monk has rented the most beautiful tour bus he could find, a $350,000 top-of-the-line model that would comfort the likes of Led Zeppelin or Styx. He wants the band to be impressed, awed, and somewhat off-balance from the start.

But he has no intention of ever using the damn thing. With the immigration problems and all the other excitement the Sex Pistols have generated, Monk expects to have some trouble getting rid of the press at the airport. He figures he'll get the band into the bus and that will be it. He's not prepared for the photographers running out and trying to follow them. Two members of the road crew look out the back window to see if they've escaped the photographers. So far so good.

The bus begins doing circles around JFK, a massive airport. After circling the airport three times (it takes that long to lose the press), the bus heads toward the Delta terminal. The Sex Pistols aren't going to spend any time in New York. They're going directly to Atlanta.

9 P.M.

Delta Flight 971 leaves for Atlanta a few minutes after nine. Cook and Jones sit together and look out the window; they're excited, they're ready to conquer America in the style of the Who and the Rolling Stones. Vicious accepts drinks from the stewardess (when he's not trying to paw her) and contents himself with a well-worn comic book; Rotten leans into the aisle, pops a pimple, and explains to anyone who will listen how boring America is.

The Americans and Brits don't talk much during the flight. Some of the Americans try to chat with Boogie (legal name: John Tiberi), a roadie they've brought over from England, but he's more interested in disseminating McLaren's Theory of Pop than discussing logistics. The security crew and the band spend most of the flight sizing up each other.

Johnston is on his own plane to Atlanta from Los Angeles. He'll meet the band and crew at the Delta terminal in Atlanta. As he heads east, he realizes his uneasy position on the tour. Because he is British, the American crew considers him an outsider; because he lives in America, the Brits on the tour are wary of him. He has to keep the peace among the factions. "They were all coming to the States with a chip on their shoulder. They spoke to me because Malcolm told them to talk to me, but they also talked to me because I was an Englishman. I had a bit more in common with them. As Englishmen, Boogie and the band had some problems with Noel because his style was so different. But they were being unrealistic. The scope of what Boogie would be doing in America was different from anything Malcolm expected of him in Europe, and Boogie didn't quite understand what he was getting into. Boogie was the sort of guy who would collect around a Svengali figure like Malcolm. Boogie was an artistic guy. I'm more straight-ahead. I was into the business—I wasn't there to kiss Malcolm's ass—and Boogie was there because he felt it was artistically right to be there. But Sid needed more help and care than Boogie could give. I'm not sure if anyone realized that."

1 A.M.

When the band arrives in Atlanta, only one reporter—a UPI stringer who has been tipped off by a cohort in New York—greets them. It's a welcome difference from the reception at JFK. For the band members, it's already 6 A.M. the next morning, but they're still excited. A less ostentatious bus meets them at the terminal (to the band members' vocal disappointment), and brings them through and past downtown to the Squire Motor Inn on Piedmont Road.

Rotten declares, "Haven't got the foggiest notion, Monk, why you didn't put on limos for us important, decadent people."

Rotten's tone is ironic, but he's half serious. The band is out to destroy the cocaine-and-limousine rock-star set and everything they stand for, but they still want to ride in style. It's the first of many contradictions about the band and how they deal with rock culture that will envelop them. Do they want the brass ring only to throw it away, or do they want to keep it and hide it so no one knows they still have it?

The Sex Pistols are staying in Atlanta, but not downtown; they're close enough to the hall that logistics the night of the show won't be difficult, and they're far enough away from the center of town so they won't be able to get into much trouble. Or so Monk thinks. As the bus pulls into the parking lot, he doesn't see Tattletale's, the strip club for bikers on the far side of the motel.

They're on the outskirts of town, just where Atlanta wants them. Keep away from our city, our stores, our women. The American music establishment—not merely factions at Warner Brothers—wants them on the outskirts, too. Regehr had to fight to get the Sex Pistols signed, and most established stars are either ignoring or attacking the young British brutes. Queen's new album, *News of the World,* features a track entitled "Sheer Heart Attack," in which they make fun of punks for being "so inarticulate."

The Sex Pistols function in an industry that doesn't want them because they challenge that industry's very core. They're in an area of the country that doesn't want them because exaggerated reports of their evil ways have preceded them. The vice squad of the Atlanta police department has been alerted by local would-be censors that the band will perform live sex acts with guns as part of their show. The police plan to attend the show in full force.

After the band settles in, Monk calls a band meeting to lay

down the rules for the tour. No one seems willing to listen. Rotten and Vicious slump in their chairs; Cook and Jones do the same sitting on the floor against the bed. McLaren is nowhere to be found: He's still in England.

"Let's listen to what Mr. Big Cigar from America has to say, boys," Rotten snarls. He turns toward Monk. "OK, Mr. Big Cigar, what else do you want us to do? What kind of good boys do you want us to be today?"

"Listen to me," Monk orders and begins to set down the tour rules, which he does with all his bands on the first night of a tour. "This is America," he says, for anyone who hasn't noticed yet. "You're on my turf. We're looking out for you. Let me show you how it works here. Go where you want to go, but take a bodyguard. This is the South. There's violence here. Don't fuck around. If you want to have a drink or smoke a joint or something, that's fine, but there will be no hard drugs on my tour."

Everyone chuckles at that one.

"If you want to do anything," Monk says, "check with me. You're in America now."

At this point, the band has had enough. "Fuck you," Vicious snaps. "We're the fucking Sex Pistols, the radical Sex Pistols. We'll do whatever we want. Who are you, American man?"

The conversation moves out to the second-floor balcony of the Squire Inn, facing into the parking lot.

"Let's get outta here," Rotten tells Vicious. "Maybe we can have some pleasure away from Mr. Big Cigar and his toy soldiers."

"All right then," Vicious responds, snapping his fingers so hard it looks like he's trying to burn off the skin.

Rotten and Vicious realize they're miles from downtown. They don't particularly want to go anywhere—it's been a long day—but they need to show the Americans who the bosses are here.

While they look over the balcony to follow Rotten and Vicious's progress, Johnston explains to Monk that the band simply doesn't understand the concept of normal touring—by McLaren's design. "Theoretically, the Sex Pistols haven't been allowed to tour in England. In fact, Malcolm never took any dates and said they were banned from touring so he could get some press. Forget being in America: Just touring is foreign to them. In fact—"

Johnston cuts off his explanation as a swirl of sound and light fills the air. "Oh shit," he swallows, looking down at Rotten and Vicious. "The fools have done it already."

Just as Rotten and Vicious leave the parking lot in the direction of Tattletale's, an Atlanta Police Department squad car screams up to them, lights flashing, sirens on. Two cops jump out. "Halt!" one yells and the policemen run twenty feet toward them. Rotten and Vicious freeze; Sid drops his bottle of vodka, which shatters on the sidewalk.

The bobbies in London are for the most part low-key, restrained, and respectful. This is their first dose of American policemen, who carry guns.

The policemen go into sarcastic-intimidation mode.

"Look, they're carrying liquor in a public area." The first policeman, who's in his mid-forties, is as big as the bodyguards Warner Brothers hired for the tour: six feet five inches tall, at least 240 pounds. His sneer runs deeper than even Vicious's; it's had two extra decades of practice.

"We could bring them in for that, couldn't we?" his partner answers. His partner is ten years older than he, six inches shorter, but just as heavy and mean-looking. "It's a city ordinance and a state law. They could be in for what, thirty days?"

"That's right, thirty days and thirty nights. They wouldn't be able to play tomorrow night if they were in jail with the murderers and rapists, would they?" He twirls his night stick as he talks, as if he were playing with a yo-yo.

"Sure wouldn't. That would be a shame, a real shame, to come all the way from England to Atlanta and not be able to play. Even worse, they'd be stuck with all those murderers and rapists. You know, sometimes they hide their weapons when we book them, bring 'em right into their jail cells. It gets ugly sometimes, when we have to pull someone out."

"You're right. You're so right," the first cop says. He cocks his gun, points it at the sky, and uncocks it. "But sometimes criminals don't even get as far as the jail. Did you read that report in the *Constitution* about guns that go off accidentally? Happens all the time. All the time."

By now, Rotten and Vicious are bewildered and terrified. They know the policemen are putting on a show for them, but they have no idea if the intimidation will be followed by real violence.

"What're ya gettin' at?" Vicious asks.

"I didn't say you could talk," the first officer snaps. His pointed finger is four inches away from Vicious's eyes. "You'll talk when I say you can."

"We didn't do nothin' wrong," Rotten says quietly.

"That's right, punk boy," says the second cop. "And you're not gonna. We're gonna be watching you boys. We heard all about you. You ain't going nowhere."

"You know, you two look like fucking retards," the first policeman chimes in. "Orange hair? Plastic pants? Why would anyone want to look like that? You should join the goddamn circus."

"Ain't nobody watching you?" asks the second policeman.

"Back at the hotel," Rotten says, and repeatedly points toward Monk and Dwayne Warner (a biker and bouncer Johnston had hired to do security; everybody calls him D.W.) on the Squire Inn balcony.

"Well, why don't you go back to them and tell them that we said to stay in your rooms and leave us good people alone. Now get the fuck out of here."

Vicious and Rotten are scared enough to keep their anger in check. They return to the hotel, looking down at their feet.

When Vicious and Rotten walk back to the second-floor balcony, Monk is grinning.

"What was that about?" Vicious asks. "They had guns on us. Guns."

"Yeah, this isn't England," Monk says. "They were just about ready to shoot you."

"You're kiddin'," Rotten shoots back. "Of course you're kidding. They wouldn't do that." He pauses for a beat. "Would they?"

"They'll blow your fucking brains out down here," Monk deadpans. "Now do you want to sit down and listen?" Monk asks.

"You ain't kidding, mate."

And for a precious few moments, Monk has some control.

2 A.M.

Before he drifts to sleep, Andy Warhol writes in his diary, "The Sex Pistols arrived in the U.S. today. Punk is going to be so big. They're so smart, whoever's running the tour, because they're starting where the kids have nothing to do, so they'll go really crazy."

CHAPTER FOUR
Day Two: Wednesday, January 4—Atlanta

9 A.M.

MONK AWAKES TO a ringing phone. A low voice, friendly but businesslike, asks, "Noel Monk?"

"Yeah?" Monk mumbles.

"I'm Tom Forcade of *High Times*."

"So?"

"I want to make a documentary of the tour."

"Oh, man, call Warner Brothers about that. I don't have anything to do with that."

The voice on the other end remains steady. After a pause, Forcade (pronounced four-sod) says, "No, Mr. Monk. I've tried that once. I didn't like it. I don't think you understand. We're going to make it worth your while."

"Really, you have to speak to Warner Brothers."

"But we want to follow you around and do a documentary of the tour. We're going to make it worth your while. Believe me."

"OK, OK," Monk says. "Call me back at twelve and then maybe we can talk. I'll get hold of Al DiMeola at Warner Brothers and find out if it's OK for you to do the video." He slams down the phone and curls back up in bed.

Monk doesn't think there was really anyone named Forcade on the phone. He assumes it's Ted Cohen playing a little trick on him. They've been on the road together many times, and they've had their fun. It's time for fun on the road again.

Monk reckons that Cohen will get the joke (Al DiMeola is a jazz-fusion guitarist who never recorded for Warner Brothers, let alone had anything to do with the company's video department), and he returns to his dreams.

At noon, Monk's phone rings again, waking him again.

"Mr. Monk?" It's a familiar voice.

"Yeah. Monk here."

"It's Tom Forcade again."

So the joke continues, Monk thinks. "Hi, Tom. How are you?" Monk does his best to sound sarcastic. Cohen is doing a great job disguising his voice, he thinks.

"Oh, I'm fine." Forcade sounds friendly in a forced way, trying to force a rapport where none exists. "What did Al DiMeola have to say about the video?"

Monk scratches his head. He is beginning to wonder if this Forcade character is for real.

"You're not fucking kidding," Monk says to Forcade.

Forcade takes a deep breath. "I do not kid, Mr. Monk. We really want to make a film. We want to make a documentary of the whole tour, get the whole story, and we're willing to pay you good money to do it. Am I making my point? Don't you know who I am?"

As he speaks, Forcade's voice speeds up, gets itself more agitated. "Tell me, am I making my point?"

Monk is still tired, and doesn't want to deal with either a joke or a crazy guy. "Fuck you. You can't buy me. Take a walk." Again, he slams down the phone and returns to his pillow.

But not for long. Barely a half hour later, Monk hears someone banging hard on his hotel-room door and he jumps up in bed. It's barely noon, Monk quickly surmises, and the Sex Pistols have already started running rampant. He jumps out of bed.

"Who is it?"

It's not any of the Sex Pistols. They're all jet-lagged, sleeping it off.

"I was sent here by Mr. Forcade, sir."

Monk throws a towel around himself. "This isn't all that

fucking funny anymore," he says through the door. "This is really insane."

"There's nothing funny, sir. I was sent here by Mr. Forcade to deliver a package."

Monk opens the door. When his eyes adjust to the bright daylight, he sees before him a tall man in chauffeur's garb. The man hands him half a dozen copies of the current issue of *High Times,* with Johnny Rotten scowling on the cover. Monk makes a tentative connection between the magazines and the phone calls, but it's fuzzy, dream-like.

"These magazines are compliments of Mr. Forcade, sir."

"Yeah, yeah."

"And your Stutz Bearcat is waiting outside in the parking lot, sir, at your convenience."

Monk looks outside past him, and beholds a beautiful Stutz Bearcat convertible in the lot.

Now Monk is mad. Either he's dealing with someone who can't take no for an answer—which seems more and more likely—or Ted Cohen is playing one of the most elaborate practical jokes Monk has seen in his decade on the road.

"Get the fuck out of my face," Monk barks to his would-be chauffeur, and slams his room door.

Monk can't fall back asleep. He showers and walks to Cohen's room.

"What the fuck are you doing?" Monk demands. "This is insane. Where'd you get that car from? I know it's my birthday." Monk says this as if he has just remembered the date himself. "But this is too much."

"What are you talking about?" Cohen asks.

Monk thinks this is tremendous, that Cohen can keep a straight face this far into the conversation.

"Come on, Teddy. Only you would spend the money and the time and the aggravation to start fun and games on the road."

Cohen draws a blank. This Forcade guy is for real; Monk must find out more about him and deal with Forcade before he becomes a real problem. But now, Monk and Cohen have to stop by the local Warner Brothers branch office. They head to the parking lot.

Between them and Cohen's rental car is the magnificent

Stutz Bearcat and the driver, who gets out of the convertible as he sees them coming.

The driver removes his hat, bows slightly, and says, "Are you ready to go, Mr. Monk?" Monk nods—then walks by. The driver replaces his hat and sits down in the driver's seat. This Monk, he thinks, must be just another one of the assholes Forcade always has him round up.

2 P.M.

Bob Merlis has scored a coup. He's gotten the Sex Pistols booked onto NBC's *Today* show, the highest-rated of the network morning infotainment programs. (In a December 21, 1977, memo about the upcoming tour to his staff Merlis wrote, "Television coverage is to be encouraged though formal interview situations with the group are dubious at best.") NBC News has sent reporter Jack Perkins to Atlanta to do an interview, so Merlis rents a suite at a posh downtown hotel for the event—he's certainly not going to let Perkins go to the Squire Inn.

As the crew sets up, the band starts giving Jack and company a good-natured hard time.

"We're so honored to be on your lovely television show," offers Rotten.

"Hey, Jack!" Jones shouts. "Give us a fiver and we'll do the interview. Let's see a fiver there."

Perkins is taken aback by the lack of decorum. "I have journalistic integrity!" he shouts back. "I do not have to pay for interviews, young man!"

Looking to avoid another Grundy ambush, the band members disperse, leaving Perkins alone with his crew. "Film this destruction!" Perkins orders.

There is none, Merlis observes. It's not a rock-star-destroyed hotel room. It's nothing, maybe an overturned can or ashtray. "Jack didn't get it all," Merlis says. "For five dollars he could have gotten a great interview. I'm sure NBC would have reimbursed him. And as for the destruction, my kids' rooms are dirtier—after they clean them."

4 P.M.

Monk and Cohen make some calls from the Warner Brothers branch office, nothing important, just some boring road logistics. The branch office is full of people trying to get radio stations to play the label's three current priority singles: Rod Stewart's "You're in My Heart," Shaun Cassidy's "Hey Deanie," and Debby Boone's "You Light Up My Life," all of which are in *Billboard*'s Top Ten singles chart. No one's bothering to make any Sex Pistols calls. Warner Brothers has twelve records, ranging from the Ramones' *Rocket to Russia* to Steve Martin's *Let's Get Small,* all selling more briskly than *Never Mind the Bollocks.* The Sex Pistols may be a priority for Bob Regehr and his commanders back in Southern California, but here in the trenches they're an afterthought.

On their way back to the hotel, Monk and Cohen stop at the Great South East Music Hall, the site of tomorrow night's show, the band's first performance in America. It's in the corner of Broadview Plaza, a large mall, next to an Oriental food store and a K mart. The Great South East is in the Buckhead section of Atlanta, several miles from downtown.

Behind the club are train tracks and a cleared area from which the road crew can load in the equipment. The band is to perform a sound check within the hour, and Monk wants to be sure all is in order. Johnston and Boogie seem to have everything under control. Everything is not as it seems.

Monk and Cohen return to the hotel. The Stutz Bearcat and driver are still in the parking lot, waiting for them.

As they return to the courtyard of the Squire Inn, Cohen says, "Watch this, birthday boy." He floors the car and stops inches from the Stutz. The driver turns white.

The driver stammers, "What are you doing, sir?"

"I'm kind of saying, get out of here," Monk offers. "I don't want you around. Tell your boss, Mr. Forcade." The driver finally leaves.

Monk and Cohen round up the band and all pile into the bus to go to the sound check. It's still a day before the show, but everyone wants the first gig to sound right.

Steve Jones walks onto the bus dressed as a stereotypical

Cool Hand Luke sheriff, wearing a big hat and big star. "I'm a cheriff!" he boasts. "I wanna see girls with big chits!"

"No problem," Cook says. "No problem."

Waiting on the bus is Bob Gruen, the photographer Warner Brothers has chosen to be the official tour chronicler. His presence means Warner Brothers can limit press interaction and still provide footage for its own promotional purposes. Gruen, a veteran rock photographer, is an ideal choice to be on the inside. He's known McLaren as far back as his days with the New York Dolls. "The first time I went to England in 1976, Malcolm was the only guy I knew to call," he says. "I took pictures of the Sex Pistols then. I went again to England in the fall of 1977. And I knew Nancy [Spungen] from New York when she was hanging out with the Dolls and the Heart-breakers. I went to see the Pistols in Atlanta. There was an extra space on the bus, and they invited me to come along. Warner Brothers paid my hotel expenses. Nobody was paying my air fare, so I stayed on the bus."

As the band members get on the bus, Monk introduces them to Heidi Robinson, a Los Angeles-based publicist for Warner Brothers who has flown in for the opening show.

Halfway to the club, Robinson weaves her way to the front of the bus. "Noel, I need to talk to you. Sid just grabbed me—you know where." She points to her crotch.

Monk apologizes profusely (although he wonders what type of reception Robinson expected) and walks back to Sid, scrunches next to him on the seat, and grins.

"You've been playing with our publicist?" Monk asks.

"Right, Monk."

Monk smiles, then quickly backhands Vicious in the stomach. Sid doubles over, more from the surprise than the pain.

"Hey, what's that for, mate?"

"You can do whatever you want to do with groupies, Sid. I don't give a shit. But if you don't treat Warner Brothers people with respect, I'll whack you again. If you're gonna grab snatch, don't do it from Warner Brothers."

The other band members are as stunned as Sid. They've never seen anything like this before. Boogie never treated anyone like this. What's all this, then?

Rotten offers his usual snarl in response. "For this we came to America? What a bloody waste."

A minute later (it's only a few miles from the hotel to the hall), the bus arrives at the Great South East Music Hall, tucked comfortably in Broadview Plaza. There's a great irony in this anarchistic band kicking off their American campaign in a sedate shopping mall, the apotheosis of America, but no one comments on it. Maybe no one comments on it because all of America seems dull. Prime-time television is full of empty comedies like *Happy Days* and *Three's Company*, and the box-office big-screen smashes of the time are *Star Wars*, escapist entertainment, and Barbra Streisand's vapid retelling of *A Star Is Born*, a film that has nothing to do with its ostensible subject, the seedy side of real-life rock and roll. Within the past twelve months, three million copies of a Farrah Fawcett poster have been sold. This is a culture bent on inertia. The Sex Pistols should be starting their American tour in a shopping mall, because America has become, to some degree, a coast-to-coast shopping mall.

It's not a particularly productive sound check as far as music is concerned, but it is the first time the entire entourage (except for McLaren) is together at the same time. Monk notices that the stage is low, barely four feet off the ground, and he worries that fans may try to rush the band.

The Americans and Brits feel each other out, trying to get comfortable. Everyone hovers around each other and the orbits get a bit closer. Red, the roadie in charge of the drums, befriends Cook. Cook gives Red precise instructions on how the drum kit should sound. Red is nonplussed. "I've never seen such a simple set in all my life. It's a piece of cake."

"No problem then?" Cook asks.

"No problem, my man."

"No problem," Jones echoes.

Red also notices a kid dressed in black, sitting in the corner, drinking. He asks Monk, "Who is this waste of time?"

"That's Boogie," Monk replies. "He's here to look after Sid."

Red stifles a laugh.

Three men stand together outside the hall trying to get

in, the only people waiting outside who aren't clearly press
representatives (there are twenty press folk here for the sound
check). These three are better-dressed but more seedy looking; their expensive clothes are brand new and incongruous.
One holds a film camera. Another, a tall, lanky, six-footer,
Monk recognizes as Mickey Rabbit. They'd worked together at
one of the rock festivals Monk helped manage when he
worked for legendary Bay Area promoter Bill Graham. With
Rabbit is a man wearing sunglasses and a cowboy hat. He's
slight, five feet six, slender, with brown hair just starting to
thin, and a well-groomed mustache. He wears tight black
pants and a western-cut jacket. In a southwestern accent, he
introduces himself to Monk as Tom Forcade.

"We called you this morning about doing this documentary," Rabbit sputters in a practiced New York grumble. "You
know, Noel, you can make a lot of money out of this. A lot of
money."

Forcade doesn't say much. He stands back and listens to
Rabbit and Monk squabble, taking mental notes on how best
to approach Monk in the future.

Monk takes the offensive. "Rabbit, I'll tell you what I told
Tom this morning. I'll tell you now. Get out of my fucking
face. If you want to do a video, call Warner Brothers. Just
leave me and the band the fuck alone."

Forcade breaks his silence. "You know, Noel, we're going
to do it whether you like it or not." Forcade smiles, more to
himself than to Monk, and tugs on the collar of his jacket.
"We're just giving you a chance to get some, uh, appreciation."

Monk returns to the club to round up the band and get
them back to the hotel. Rounding up the four of them takes
half an hour. They leave the small hall full of smoke and
spilled beer. As they barge out, Monk tells one of the security
guards to walk five feet in front of the entourage, latch onto
Mickey Rabbit's camera, and pretend he's trying to twist off
the lens. A little intimidation never hurt anyone, Monk thinks.
He also realizes that these people are for real, and if he
doesn't deal with them soon they're going to make this a very
long tour.

1 A.M.

Ted Cohen made a mistake earlier this evening. The Warner Brothers artist-development man offered to take the band members out to dinner. "I can handle the boys," he'd boasted. "I have it under control."

He brings them to the local Scotch and Sirloin, and holds court in a private back room. Monk is pretty sure Cohen is in over his head with the band at a restaurant, but his friend won't be deterred.

Monk insists that members of the security crew accompany the group; Cohen agrees. Monk instructs the security men to sit back, relax, and let whatever will happen happen. He returns to his room, showers, and goes out to dinner with an old friend. It is a pleasant break, quiet and relaxing.

When Cohen and the band return, Ted looks mortified.

"Hi, Teddy," Monk mocks. "Did you have a good time?" Cohen is too distraught to respond.

"What happened?" Monk asks.

"What didn't happen, Noel? That's the question." Hmm, Monk thinks. Ted usually doesn't talk this loud. "What didn't happen? They're animals, Noel, fucking animals. We had the guy from Warner Publishing there, and they trashed the guy from head to foot. Johnny dipped his tie in water and tried to make spikes out of the guy's hair with butter. Sid spackled his tie and jacket with ketchup and made believe he was going to barf on him. Johnny stuck tissues deep into his nose and then threw them at the guy."

"So what are you talking about?" Monk asks. "What's the problem? They're a bunch of good rock and rollers."

"They threw everything. They cursed at the waiter. Steve and Paul starting filling the publishing guy's shoes with food, so the guy left. I can't believe these guys."

"Teddy, I thought you said you had it under control."

Cohen isn't finished with his litany. "Red taught them how to flip butter off their spoons onto the ceiling. They had twenty pounds up there waiting to drip."

"That's a real fun thing to do, Teddy." Monk has heard worse. It didn't sound like a big deal.

It is a big deal. D.W. was part of the dinner party and had gone to the restaurant bathroom, where he was confronted by Sid. Sid, skinny, shaky drunk, starts taunting big, brawny D.W. Sid doesn't know that his bodyguard hung out with bikers for the better part of a decade.

"You're one of the fucking bodyguards, huh?"

"Yeah," D.W. answers, throwing away a paper towel. "I'm going to look after you." His tone isn't condescending, just matter-of-fact, it's his job.

Sid takes another swig of peppermint schnapps, belches, and says, "You think you're a tough guy, don't you? You're a hard knocker, ain't you?"

"Yeah." Is this going to be a problem?

Sid rests the schnapps bottle in the sink. "Well, if you're so fucking tough, why don't you just take me on?" He lunges at D.W.

This is insane, D.W. thinks. He's not about to get into a fight with the person he's being paid to protect. Word of Sid's heroin habit had preceded him from England, although no one on the American side—including Rory—had been clued in to how bad it had been raging. The whole point of having Boogie on the tour, after all, is to have one person whose only job is to look after Sid.

D.W. takes a deep breath and lets Sid hit him for a few minutes. He's drunk, he's wiry. How much can it hurt?

It can hurt plenty. Finally, when Sid's punches start to connect and add up to real pain, D.W. stares at Sid and announces, "That was your turn, you fucking limey. Now it's my turn." He gathers his strength, pulls Sid off him, grabs him by his hair, and bangs his head—hard—against the sink one, two, half a dozen times. Sid slumps to the tiled floor. He'd come into the bathroom looking to punch someone, looking to get punched. He's gotten what he wanted.

Sid breathes fast and hard, and cradles his head. "OK, OK, enough. You're good enough. I like you. Now we can be friends." Dazed from the battle and the compliment, D.W. leaves the bathroom, Sid crumpled on the floor.

It's only the first night of the tour, what's supposed to be the easy part. There have been no shows, no long travel days, no opportunities to go truly wild. Yet already the band members and the crew have resorted to violence. The tension that takes weeks to accumulate on most rock tours has already reached a fever pitch. Everyone from the paparazzi to Forcade wants a piece of the band, and all they can do to fight back is to go after the people who are supposed to be on their side. Who's the enemy now?

A few minutes after Sid staggers out of the restaurant bathroom, he starts taunting Camel, another member of the security force. Camel refuses to fight and pushes Sid aside.

3 A.M.

Sid is safely back in his room at the Squire Inn, nursing his second or third or tenth peppermint schnapps. The rest of the band members are amok in Atlanta, traveling across after-hours discos and transvestite bars. Rotten, Jones, and Cook aren't getting into any serious trouble, but they are being initiated into America. They're club-hopping from disco to disco; they're discovering 1978 America.

D.W. reports to Monk what happened in the restaurant bathroom, and Monk walks into Sid's room to try to make sense of it. Sid is on the bed, lying on top of the covers, propped up on two pillows, drinking yet another peppermint schnapps (he hasn't yet begun to partake of Monk's Valiums), staring through the television, begging for smack. Right now the schnapps is all that separates Vicious from even more severe heroin withdrawal. It's a necessary evil.

On his left arm, below his three-inch-wide spiked leather band, Sid wears a watch, which makes no sense. It's debatable whether he can tell time, but it's a sure thing he wouldn't care even if he could. What makes sense is that it's not his watch. It's Rory's. He has stolen it from Johnston's room, and he'll use it to buy junk as soon as he gets the chance.

"Sid, I just talked to D.W. What's going on here, man?"

"Noel, I like D.W. He's a good man. He can fight. That's the kind of guy I want around me."

Monk nods. Vicious bonds with people by fighting with

them. A typical street scruff, no major problem if you don't add in the smack situation. But how can you leave it out?

Sid takes another swig, sinks deeper into his pillow, and continues. "But Camel, man, Camel ain't no fucking friend of mine. Yeah, I asked Camel to fight with me. He said he couldn't fight with me, but after the tour was over he'd blow my fucking brains out. That's a chickenshit thing to say. He's fucking worthless. I don't want him around me."

"How about I put him on the stage crew and take him off your security?"

"I like that, Monk. Hey, want some schnapps?"

They swig from the same bottle.

CHAPTER FIVE
Day Three: Thursday, January 5—Atlanta

6 P.M.

A LARGE SEX PISTOLS DISPLAY at the local Peaches shop is being broken down by one of the record-store chain's regional sales representatives. When asked why, he says he hates the group. "Do I need any other reason?"

Back at the Squire Inn, Johnston and Monk discuss logistics for the evening's show, but they might as well be talking in different languages. They serve different masters: Johnston is there to enforce McLaren's whims and facilitate creative anarchy within limits; Monk is there to satisfy the Warner Brothers executives and keep the tour smooth and close to budget. Rarely do the twain meet.

"They don't agree on anything," says Bob Gruen. "They could both be looking at the same thing. One person says they're looking at an apple; the other says they're looking at a horse."

Johnston is taken aback by the way the tour is progressing, even in areas that don't start with Monk. When Johnston met the band at the hotel Tuesday night, the first thing they felt they had to tell him was how much they hate each other and McLaren. It's hard to marshal the forces if they won't fight together. (Although he has grave reservations about Monk's methods, Johnston is glad he's there. Johnston has to worry about all aspects of the band's career; it's helpful to

have someone managing the day-to-day tour arrangements.)
And Sid is starting to act irrational.

Merlis confirms this when he rides in the bus with the
band to the hall. Once, when the bus stops for a red light, Sid
bolts out the door and one of the bodyguards has to retrieve
him before he runs away. Sid is trying to run away to get
drugs. Johnston still hasn't discovered the location of the
watch his father gave him.

At the Great South East, Monk talks to Glen Allison, who
runs the hall. Glen and Monk are old friends; they've worked
together many times on many tours. Allison has heard that
Monk is looking for one more security guard. He volunteers
for the job. "It'll give me an excuse to get out of town for a
spell," he says.

"I wanna be on this fucking tour," Allison tells Monk. "It
sounds great, lots of fun."

"You're big enough," Monk says to his six feet five, 280
pound friend. "You can keep it under control. Come along."

Glen's wife Betty will also come. A veteran road rat herself, she'll be like one of the guys. Monk usually isn't comfortable with women traveling with a band, "but I figured Betty
would be a calming influence."

Also at the hall, the Sex Pistols meet Doreen Cochran, age
twenty, who works at the club. She fancies herself a punk bon
vivant and she is trying to find a way to make a living as a
manager of a rock-and-roll band. She and her boyfriend, Dan
Baird (who plays guitar for a local band, the Nasty Bucks),
have immersed themselves in all things punk, playing Sex
Pistols and Ramones records over and over.

Baird draws a line at what punk he'll allow on the family
turntable. "I don't go for the Damned and Dead Boys, because
they're the theater end of punk. They want to dress up bad
and scare Mom. Big deal. The Pistols are real rock and roll.
That's what I want."

Cochran, who works in the restaurant that adjoins the
Great South East Music Hall, has been at the hall since 9 A.M.
waiting for the band to show up, although she knows they
won't be in until late afternoon. She's that excited. Doreen is
no stranger to wild entertainment—she has an act in which
she dresses up as "Cheryl Doreen, the Rodeo Queen." She's

spent time with unusual people—she went to high school with Mark David Chapman—but the Sex Pistols are unprecedented in their weirdness. She doesn't want to miss a second.

When the band shows up, Cochran isn't looking where she's going and literally walks into Rotten.

"Sorry. Excuse me." In a way, she is reluctant to meet Rotten and his ilk. She's curious, enthralled by the rock business, but wary. She's fascinated by the whole thing, but not in a sexual sense. As she told a friend, "They probably don't call him Rotten for nothing."

Rotten's bullshit detector is quite sensitive. He can see immediately that Doreen is a true fan, not some record-company wanker, so he shuts off his sneer for a bit.

"Dear, can ya tell me where a man might get 'imself a lager?"

Cochran is star-struck. Her fascination with the way Rotten looks isn't sexual, but he does look different from anyone she might normally see around Brookhaven. She seems to forget for a second where the bar is, but quickly snaps back. "Uh, that's where I'm going right now. I'm going that way. Uh, wanna come?"

Rotten follows her to the bar, as does Vicious. She gets them all drinks and leads the small talk. Sid drools.

"There's gonna be a big turnout tonight," Cochran offers.

"Oh yes, the lovely American press," Rotten counters. "They must be waiting for us desperately, unless they've found something new to write about pet rocks."

Sid says nothing. He has nodded out on his stool, his face in his drool. Monk walks by and decides it's time for Rotten and Vicious to go back to the hotel. Sid doesn't respond to his request, so Monk yanks Sid off the bar stool by his belt loop. Sid wakes up.

8 P.M.

Monk and Johnston carry on a running disagreement over to the room Sid is sharing with Boogie. Boogie, the man who is supposed to be looking after Sid, is nowhere in sight, so

Monk and Johnston decide to stick around and keep an eye on their prized bass player. If nothing else, it's something they can agree upon. The phone rings. Sid reaches to answer it, and Noel yanks the phone wires out of the wall. No one is going to get to Sid. He positions one of his security guards outside Sid's room to make sure he doesn't disappear before they leave for the show around ten o'clock.

Down the hall in Room 309, Rotten is entertaining guests, among them Cochran. He has surrounded himself with an assortment of sycophants, weirdoes, and real fans. He's holding court. He signs a press photo, "I look like a cunt in this photo." He borrows Doreen's big wig—the one she uses when she transforms herself into Cheryl Doreen—and prances around the room, calling himself Dolly Rotten. He puts on a front, acting like he's in a fine mood, but he's not. Besides, anyone can join in on this party. Today's Atlanta *Journal* reported that the band is staying at the Squire Inn.

At the same time, Cook and Jones are in Tattletale's, getting more and more drunk. Tonight's show is the most important show of the Sex Pistols' career, and everyone is profoundly nervous. Everyone except for McLaren. He's flying first class from New York to Atlanta, relaxing and scheming.

10 P.M.

No one feels like standing up, let alone putting on an energetic show. Those who aren't still jet-lagged have hangovers. All the Sex Pistols are worrying about the evening's performance, the band's American debut. As much as they try to seem cynical about their career, they do want to go over well. Contradictions begin to multiply.

Day-of-show jitters enveloping them, the band files into the bus for the show. It takes forty-five minutes to get the four band members the two hundred feet from their rooms to the bus.

The bus pulls to the back of the hall. In front, the line stretches past the K mart. The lucky six hundred with tickets (which were distributed with safety pins stuck in them) are joined by hundreds more curiosity seekers. The clothes are dour, but the mood is ebullient. Young women flash their chests toward the television cameras. Bob Merlis sells his press tickets to the American journalists, but dozens of British journalists have also appeared. Merlis won't help them. He doesn't want to help the Sex Pistols sell records in England. The Sex Pistols are on a different label in England, and he is a company man. One Fleet Street reporter sent him flowers during the day, but Merlis holds fast. They all find a way to get in.

Cochran and Baird, who are near the front of the line, are amazed by the turnout. They expected a crowd, but nothing like this. Cochran thinks this is what it must be like to be a vampire. You don't know there are lots of people like you until you fly around at night and meet them.

The hall isn't ideal for hard rock. It was designed in 1974 as a room for folk music. It's a rectangular room with the stage in the middle of one of the long walls. Performers like Jerry Garcia, Doc and Merle Watson, Randy Newman, and Ry Cooder have played here. But when full bands come in, the music blasts hard at the short wall. On the sides, all you hear are the echoes off the short wall. (In general, Atlanta isn't getting the prime rock acts. Recent visitors in town have included Hot Tuna and the pre-comeback Kinks. Atlanta usually gets the established, second-level fodder.)

The seating arrangements in the Great South East aren't ideal for tonight, either. Instead of seats, the floor is lined by long benches that aren't secured tightly. The hall isn't oversold too badly, but everyone is cramming toward the front. The heat is made worse by the intense bright lights from the television cameras—and the stage lights aren't even on yet. People are posing for the cameras inside, too. Two men show off their pierced nipples for the cameras. Until the music starts, the Sex Pistols invasion is more a fashion event than a musical event. It's a pity McLaren hasn't set up a concession stand with Sex paraphernalia. He'd do well.

Several people from Warner Brothers have flown in for the gig, but none of them wants to be around the band except Ted Cohen. (Even after the restaurant incident, he'd probably rather be with the band members than anyone from National

Record Mart.) Carl Scott doesn't even want the band members to know who he is.

Before the band and crew enter the club, Monk and Johnston notice that Forcade and his film crew are by the stage door to meet them. The Sex Pistols' entrance will be preserved on film.

"That film crew doesn't come in," Monk tells Allison.

"No problem, Noel. No problem."

"You don't seem to be going along with us," Forcade calls to Monk as the band files by. "Why don't you go along with us?"

The group keeps walking. "You have to at least treat us with respect!" Forcade shouts as Monk slips out of earshot. Forcade has a thin, tight build, he's wearing a suit, and his hair and moustache are immaculate. He looks a lot like Monk.

The band and crew walk backstage. Allison, imposing with his thick arms crossed, sticks around to keep an eye on Forcade and the cameramen.

The film crew may be under control for now, but Monk gets a new surprise when he enters the lobby of the Great South East. He's met by three vice-squad cops, one from Atlanta and two from Memphis, the next stop on the tour. The middle-aged men are worried. They've heard the rumors, they know the band's reputation. If anything immoral is going to happen, they are going to take swift and strong action.

Monk has to explain that what they think is going to happen is not going to happen. He has to convince them that the band is providing ample security, or the law will step in. It's a good thing he's wearing a suit; he needs to impress upon these people that he's legitimate and trustworthy. A ripped T-shirt wouldn't be helpful.

The cops confront Monk with their reports. Monk turns on his portable Norelco to play it safe. Charges fly.

"We hear they're beating each other with whips," says Lieutenant R. B. Howell of the Memphis police department's special investigation unit.

"I heard they jump into the audience and beat the shit out of the people," says Clyde W. Keenan, a legal officer for the Department.

"I heard they pull a woman onstage and rape her."

"We hear there's throwing up onstage and into the crowd."

"I heard they fuck each other up the ass."

"Any simulated masturbation or anything like that will be dealt with."

Monk finally gets a word in. "Men, this is just plain old rock and roll with a new twist. It's nothing to worry about. Go to Tattletale's if you want that stuff. You'll see a lot more nudity there than you'll see here."

The charges grow picayune. Within three minutes, Monk and the policemen haggle over the legal nuances between band members vomiting onto the crowd and band members vomiting on each other.

Monk calms the officers, but is left uneasy. Now he knows what the establishment in the South expects from the Sex Pistols. If McLaren wants to be where the trouble is, he couldn't have picked a better region.

The South isn't ready for the Sex Pistols, but maybe the South needs a dose of them. It wouldn't be the first time they needed to be rattled. Although rock and roll is a massive, respectable business nowadays, it wasn't that long ago that the South, the birthplace of rock and roll, was also a battlefield.

"The obscenity and vulgarity of the rock-and-roll music is obviously a means by which the white man and his children can be driven to the level with the nigger," said the executive secretary of the Alabama White Citizens Council around the time Elvis Presley was starting to make waves outside Memphis. Rock and roll was born in the South, screaming for its life against racism and a fistful of narrow-minded notions. Tonight, the scream is back.

The opening act at the Great South East is called Merc-o-Matic, a frat-rock band with proto-psychedelic leanings. They're not completely useless—they seem as anxious for a laugh as anyone in the crowd—but don't try to impress that on the capacity crowd, which is getting hotter and more anxious for the headliners. The press doesn't respond well, either. A local fanzine dismisses them: "Forget the opening band. We'll refer to them from now on as the Shitheads."

11 P.M.

For their first show in America, the Sex Pistols are driving to hell as fast as they can. The band members come alive when the stage lights hit them. In that way, they are show-business professionals.

Cook pounds his drums so hard he seems to be rising from his seat, Jones sprays windmill riffs at the crowd, Vicious pogos, spits, and occasionally gets around to slapping random strings on his bass guitar. The button on his T-shirt reads, I'M A MESS. Rotten, still wearing his green plaid jacket, leans over the crowd, taunting them with his lyrics, his stage patter, and his stares. They kick off with their antianthem "God Save the Queen," chanting its key line—"No future for you!"—over and over as the crowd screams along. They share their anger; there's enough to go around.

"You can all stop staring now," Rotten spits after the opening song deteriorates. "We're ugly and we know it. Just relax and have some fun."

The front of the crowd responds to this by throwing pig's noses and pig's feet onstage. This is, after all, the South. Maybe one fourth of the crowd are real punks; most are there to be part of the show.

The stripped-down, raw music the Sex Pistols tear through is available nowhere else. Other popular bands of the moment have gained their stature through superior musicianship, a skill all but useless to the Sex Pistols. Members of bands like Yes and Led Zeppelin pride themselves on their technical ability, but the Sex Pistols' attitude is that technical proficiency in and of itself is useless. What matters is the feeling of a direct song. Their music is purposefully sloppy.

McLaren, who's nowhere to be found at the Great South East (his flight just got into Atlanta, and he's back—cool and comfortable—at the Squire Inn), certainly encourages this sound and this attitude, but he doesn't have to force-feed it. Johnny Rotten isn't just the band's mouthpiece. He's its raging brain. McLaren or his friend Jamie Reid might drop a word like "anarchy" or "vacant" that Rotten seizes upon and turns into a manifesto, but McLaren is not the Svengali to Rotten he'd like to be perceived as. McLaren thought he was working with a tabula rasa, but he soon found out that Rotten has ideas of his own—pointed, forbidden ideas. McLaren's genius is marketing, not music, so he's content to have another mind at work—for now. The name Sex Pistols, which is sufficient for many to come to the Great South East tonight, is perfect for McLaren's vision, in that it's an outrageous monicker that means nothing. In the most hedonistic times, when all-night cocaine-and-sex orgies at Studio 54 are many people's dreams, the name of the band foreshadows a time when sex might become a very scary proposition. No fun.

No one's thinking about this right now. The music is too loud and the club is too hot and filled with intermingling sweat and beer. Roadies keep handing Steve Jones new guitars, each of which is slightly further out-of-tune than the previous one. Vicious is emaciated, white-skinned, living up to the image of what people want him to look like. Yet it is Rotten who deserves to hold center stage. He is as direct as any performer in the history of rock and roll. He dares his audience to stare back. He makes unimaginable moves. He does a little hunkered-over dance. He sits on the drum riser and scowls, then jumps into the air and rants.

Through all this, he's showered with debris from the audience. "Oh, thank you. Gifts. Lovely. Just lovely."

1 A.M.

Backstage at the Great South East, band and crew relax. Nobody got hurt, nothing went wrong. They drink extensively, smoke a few joints. Things feel good. They feel good. Jones relaxes with a blond woman who identifies herself to local reporters as a "free-lance hairdresser."

Rotten, Cook, Jones, and their entourage decide to see the town. They stop briefly at a club called Victoria Station but leave quickly. Johnny notes the irony: "All the way across the fuckin' ocean and you bring me to fuckin' Victoria Station."

Their next stop is the Locker Room, a private, all-night club that caters primarily to transvestites and female impersonators. At the Locker Room, Johnny starts to open up to

Cochran. Gradually, the talk shifts from childhood re-
membrances to rambling about the state of England. "To hell
with the BBC. There's no freedom of the press back in England, no freedom of the press on dear old Fleet Street. No
jobs, no work, no freedom."

Rotten takes another swig of ale and tries to move the talk
a few steps closer to a real conversation. "What's wrong with
these kids?" he asks Cochran with a twinge of genuine con-
cern. "They didn't get to the stage. They didn't even try. They
just stood there."

Cochran is surprised. England must be so different.
"They're not into 'God Save the Queen' here," she says. "It's
different here. We all have jobs, even if we don't like 'em. Why
are you singing 'Anarchy in the U.K.'? This is the U.S.A. How
about some anarchy here?"

Still, Cochran saw things from a different perspective.
"That was the most frenzied crowd I've ever seen," she says.
"You really got them going."

"In England," Rotten says, with more than a trace of
boosterism, "they'd have gotten to the stage."

Rotten excuses himself to the next table and almost immediately begins to receive a blow job from a drag queen on all
fours who's been hanging on his every word.

The queen looks up at the voice of the Sex Pistols. "Ah,
you're not so rotten after all." Johnny urinates in her mouth.

Steve Jones leans over to Cochran. "Are all women in
America like you?"

"I hope not," she says, and looks away.

2 A.M.

Backstage at the Great South East, the crew and Vicious,
the only band member still at the hall, are getting along well.
The previous night's violence seems like an icebreaking aber-
ration.

"It's nice to relax," sighs Allison. "Today has been a
bitch." All sink deeper into their seats.

Out of nowhere, Sid runs out the back door, into the

darkness. Allison sprints after him and quickly retrieves him. Sid is shaking; the heroin withdrawl is starting to hit hard.

"I've got to go out and get something," Vicious repeats in a low voice, like a mantra. "I've got to go out and get something. I've got to go out and get something."

After he all but inhales a pint of vodka, Sid seems relaxed and everyone once again lets their guard down a bit. Sid takes this as a cue to bolt. He disappears along the railroad tracks behind the club. Glen jumps up and runs after him.

Half an hour later, Glen returns—without Sid.

"Where's Sid?"

"I don't know. I lost him."

Monk is furious, but he has to maintain control. "Well, we have a plane to Memphis to catch tomorrow at noon," he barks. "I'm going to leave you here. You've gotta find him. The only one on the crew who knows Atlanta is you. You know what he's looking for."

By now, the rest of the crew is in the bus waiting to go back to the hotel, so Monk hops on and rides back. He doesn't tell anyone Sid is missing.

When he gets back to the hotel, Monk goes to Johnston's room to inform him of Vicious's disappearance. Johnston is not there, leaving Monk to meet a beret-topped McLaren. They exchange wary felicitations.

Monk is confused. "I didn't see you at the show, Malcolm."

"Oh, I couldn't go to the show. I couldn't do that." McLaren toys with a smile but loses interest and returns to a blank expression.

Monk is still confused. He's also angry that McLaren is the press's darling and wasn't at his own band's American debut. "Why didn't you come to the show?"

"Well, uh, there could have been a riot." McLaren lets his voice rise a notch, still in control. "I could have gotten hurt. I didn't want to be in the middle of all that."

"No, no," Monk counsels, about to burst. "The show went fine. Just fine. You should've been there."

Monk picks McLaren up from his chair by his lapels. McLaren is too shocked to respond; he goes limp.

"You sonofabitch," Monk seethes. "They're your own

fucking band, you wanted to play every difficult southern date where there could have been trouble, and you didn't have the fucking balls to even show up at the show. You call yourself a manager?"

"I'm a manager," McLaren offers softly. "Just different from what you lot are used to."

Monk pushes McLaren against the wall and lets him go. He looks both ways, darting his head back and forth, and says quietly, "Malcolm, there's someone out to get you."

Malcolm composes himself and asks who.

"Don't worry, Malky, don't worry. I'll protect you." Monk turns away in disgust and leaves.

The band's manager refuses to deal with his band, the road manager has assaulted the manager, and one of the band members is lost thousands of miles from home, somewhere in Atlanta's underworld, looking for a fix. The tour has begun.

Johnny strikes a classic pose.

Noel guides Sid offstage after the Longhorn show.

Paul poses in his hotel room.

Busy man Steve shows the photographer how it's done.

ROBERTA BAYLEY

The Sex Pistols onstage

Johnny and Sid pose; Glen Allison looks for an escape hatch.

Noel at work. The smile indicates that the tour is still in its first days.

The San Antonio show, as those in the back of the crowd saw it

No, Paul didn't drink from all those beer cans. That's what the floor of Randy's Rodeo looked like after the show.

Sid holds court.

Every band needs a mascot.

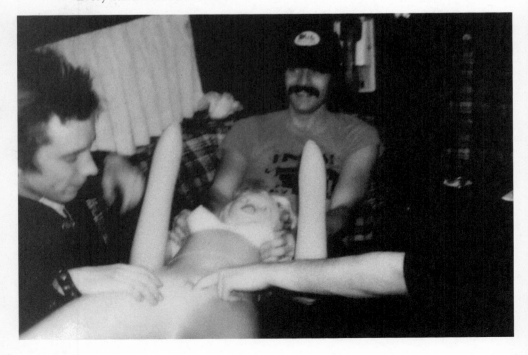

John, the artist, watches the miles roll by.

The face that launched ten thousand spiked haircuts

Charles the bus driver wonders if Sid really wants him to join the band.

Noel, happy to be outside the bus

After the Kingfish show,
Sid shares his warmth.

Onstage at Cain's ballroom

CHAPTER SIX

Day Four: Friday, January 6—Memphis

Noon

SID IS STILL MISSING. The band has no choice but to fly to Memphis without him, and hope that Allison gets lucky.

They have to go to Memphis. They have no contingency plans: What contingency plans could there be? They know that if they don't find Vicious by the time of the show that night at the Taliesyn Ballroom, there isn't going to be a tour. It will be the end of the tour, as well as everybody's reputation.

On Delta Flight 350 out of Atlanta, the band and crew sit on the left side of the aisle; on the right side, thirty reporters and photographers lay in wait. Right after the plane takes off, one short English tabloid reporter walks over to Rotten and says, "I want to do an interview with you boys, all right?"

Rotten tells Monk that no one in the band will talk to a British reporter.

"Oh, we hate them, the bloody fools," Rotten says. "Those poseurs, they don't know a good thing. They don't know a bad thing. They're just a bunch of fucking wankers."

The Fleet Street tabloids have treated the Sex Pistols as something of a joke, but a joke to be abhorred, wiped from the face of the earth. One paper paid homage to McLaren's swindles by awarding the quartet the honor of being "England's Young Businessmen of the Year." Nonetheless, the tabloids also follow the group's every move: Sex Pistols news, however distasteful, sells newspapers.

"You've got a point there, Johnny," Monk notes. "If that's what you want, fine. No problem."

"I'm sorry," Monk tells the reporter. "I talked to the boys and we can't help you out. Would you please go back to your seat? You're disturbing these people."

"What? Go back to my seat?" the reporter asks. "Pardon me, sir. I wasn't aware that you owned Delta Airlines."

"Sir," Monk responds, holding his distaste in check. "We own the whole fucking country. You're a guest. Now sit down and shut up."

Unwilling to force the issue just yet, the reporter returns to his seat. Monk watches the reporter sit down and notices someone in the seat behind the reporter. Tom Forcade waves. Monk glares and looks away. He wants to catch up on some of the sleep he lost. He was up nearly all night worrying, planning.

Fifteen minutes out of Memphis, a lightning bolt flashes by the left side of the plane and shakes it a bit. So much for sleep. Rotten turns even whiter than usual. He hasn't flown much and isn't used to the occasional meteorological incident.

Monk enjoys the sight. "Johnny, I thought you were a nihilist," he says. "I thought you didn't worry about anything."

"Bloody hell I don't," Rotten retorts. "What the fuck was that? Shit, I don't want to fucking fly again."

Monk leans back. "Don't worry, Johnny. I don't think we're going to be flying a whole lot."

2 P.M.

In Memphis, the band heads out in a rented city bus to visit Graceland; they want to see Elvis's house. It's a few days shy of his first birthday as a dead legend, and they want to join the celebration outside his estate. The three present band members, especially Rotten, are fans of Elvis, or at least fans of the idea of young Elvis, the Elvis who stormed out of the Sun Recording Service. The Sex Pistols are also fascinated that someone so young and powerful could have destroyed himself so utterly and senselessly—even if Elvis's flame-out isn't as spectacular or romantic as the James Dean kind (the kind McLaren is pushing on Vicious).

Rotten is the only Sex Pistol who gets more than just a kitschy kick from the journey. He's learned how pop's star-making machinery works and how the Sex Pistols are being made to function as part of that machinery. He looks toward the grave and knows that Elvis's future is one potential future for them. It must be better to burn out than to fade away, he's certain, and he walks by. It won't happen to me.

At the Holiday Inn, the crew notices that the press entourage is checking in, too. Monk realizes that the press has the band's itinerary (as at JFK, they took a circuitous route from the airport to lose those following them); this will be the last previously scheduled hotel at which the band actually stays.

Monk checks the Sex Pistols into the hotel and takes his bags to the elevator. He notices a familiar face riding in the elevator beside him.

"Hello, Noel," says Forcade. "Nice to see you. Lovely weather, don't you think? See you at the show tonight." Forcade is trying to appear as a discreet businessman, but he's clearly agitated. He wants to scream at Monk, throttle him a bit, but that wouldn't be good business, so he stays put.

Monk smiles. "I hope not."

The elevator stops. "Oh, you will," Forcade says. "Have a nice day. Oh, and please give Sid my best." The elevator doors shut behind him.

4 P.M.

In his room, Monk gets the first good news of the day. Allison has just arrived from Atlanta, and he's got Vicious, who's in relatively good shape.

Boogie and Monk walk downstairs to claim Sid. On the way down, Monk tells Boogie, "Don't lose him. Don't let him out of your sight. He's your responsibility. And make him take a damn bath."

"Oh yeah, no problem, mate," says Boogie. "I'll do it, it's m'job. That's what I'm here for. I'll take care of him." Boogie walks Sid to the elevator. Sid is barely conscious; he puts up no fight.

Allison won't tell Monk how he found Sid, but Noel doesn't care. He's grateful to have his bass player back. No questions asked. Monk doesn't want to know. If Allison did tell Monk where he found Vicious, Monk might not find his ignorance so blissful.

Vicious, as expected, had run away from the Great South East in search of a fix. Bands with junkies have an instant reputation in every town they invade, and the Sex Pistols are no exception. Vicious had planned a rendezvous and he wasn't going to be denied, even if he had to run away.

After he was safely away from Noel's security people, Sid began to make his way to a house just a few blocks away from Broadview Plaza. It's a direct route, straight a few blocks and one left turn.

Sid promptly got lost. He disappeared from the hall in the wrong direction and it took him an hour and a half to negotiate the half-dozen blocks to his connection.

When Sid arrived at his new friend's home, he didn't talk much. He hadn't shot up in nearly four days and his tolerance for small talk was lower than usual. Within five minutes, he had turned over Johnston's watch, endured an endless wait of thirty or forty seconds, plunged the needle into his arm, and felt the rush.

Sid nodded out soon after the heroin took, but by 3 A.M. he was awake and antsy. He explored his surroundings, picked up a bottle of vodka, and quickly found a set of kitchen knives. Bored, anxious for some action, Sid took one of the knives to himself. Using a mirror as a guide, Sid carved I WANNA FIX across his chest. Sid wasn't alarmed to see the blood dripping and congealing, but his nominal host was. He rushed Sid to Piedmont Hospital on Peachtree Road.

In the early morning hours, just as he was about to lose hope, Glen rechecked the hospitals and got lucky at 1968 Peachtree. Whether it was lucky for Sid to be checked out of the hospital and brought to Memphis to continue the tour is another story.

9 P.M.

Monk has been able to squeeze in a short nap. He calls the crew at the night's venue, the Taliesyn Ballroom on Union Avenue (that's right, just down the road from the legendary Sun Studios, the birthplace of rock and roll). Everything is proceeding close to schedule, the opening act (Quo Junior, a group led by Eddie Floyd's old bass player and featuring a Hendrix-disciple guitarist named Velvet Turner) is about to go on. It's time for the band to come over.

Monk rounds up Johnny, Steve, and Paul, and asks D.W. to get Boogie and Sid. D.W. comes back with a confused, drunken Boogie, who says, "I haven't seen Sid for two hours. I don't know what happened to him. We were having a beer, and he left."

"You fucking idiot," Monk snaps. "You stupid sonofa-bitch. We've lost Sid twice in two days."

As far as Monk can see, Boogie is too drunk to be of any help to him. At that moment, he decides to take Boogie out of Sid's room. From now on Monk will stay with Sid. Boogie can do something unimportant—like the band's sound.

Monk stands in the lobby, baffled. Rotten, Cook, and Jones sprawl across the lobby couches, perturbed. "It's the smack garbage again," Rotten says. "Smack smack smack. I wish Sidney would just start taking care of himself and let us move on. He's holdin' us back, you know."

"You think you've problems," Cook offers. "Try playing drums with someone who can't play a fuckin' note on his bass."

"Maybe we should get Glen back," Jones wonders aloud.

"Oh, that would be wonderful," Rotten sneers. "And if he's not available, we'll get his twin brother Paul McCartney. Perhaps his wife can add keyboards and arrange strings for us."

Once again, Vicious has disappeared. But this time, Monk has no one who's familiar enough with the city to find him. As in Atlanta, they're staying away from the center of the city. Their Holiday Inn, just off Route 55, is in an industrial section of Memphis, near the airport. It's wide open, an easy area in which to get lost if you want to.

Monk doesn't have too much time to ruminate, because he's just been paged. He picks up the house phone.

"Noel?"

"Yeah."

"It's Ted Cohen. I'm at the gig. We've got a major problem happening here."

"What's happening, Teddy?"

"It looks like they oversold the gig big time. There are hundred of kids with tickets who can't get in and they're all pretty pissed off. I just talked to a cop, and he told me that the city SWAT team is on the way."

Monk feels a tap on his shoulder. It's the man at the reception desk. "Mr. Monk, you have another call. He says it's urgent."

"Teddy, I've got problems of my own here," Monk says into the phone. "I'll get there as soon as I can."

Monk places the receiver back on the phone and waits for the front desk to ring through the second call. When he picks up the phone, he hears a voice that has become all too familiar.

"Mr. Monk? This is Mr. Forcade. I believe you're missing someone, aren't you?"

"Yeah. Wait—you know where Sid is?"

"Maybe. Maybe not."

"You motherfucker."

Forcade chuckles. "Now don't be nasty, Noel. Don't be nasty. Let's think about what we can do. If you come to my room by yourself, we can talk—about my documentary, that is, and then perhaps the two of us will have an opportunity to talk about where Sidney is."

Forcade's tone makes clear that he's no longer asking for permission; he's merely dictating terms. "I repeat, you are to come by yourself. I assume that I've made myself clear." Forcade recites his room number and looks forward to a meeting with Monk on his own terms.

Monk writes down the room number, grabs D.W. and a house security man, and runs to Forcade's room. The band members sit in the lobby, looking away, in their own worlds, oblivious to Monk's difficulties.

In their haste, Monk, D.W., and the hotel security guard

barrel down two halls like Keystone Cops on meth until they finally find the right door.

Monk pushes the security guards to the side and knocks on Forcade's door.

Through the door, he hears, "Are you Noel?"

"Yes."

"Are you alone?"

"Of course. I'm a man of my word."

Forcade opens the door and the three of them charge in. Forcade is appalled. "You're not alone," he notices.

"Eat shit," Monk spits. "Where the fuck is Sid?"

Monk is cocky, but he's also worried. He's done his homework on Thomas K. Forcade, and he doesn't like what he's found out.

Forcade was born in 1945 and grew up in the Southwest. He attended the University of Utah until 1967 when he came to New York and helped put together the Underground Press Syndicate, an umbrella group for 150-odd alternative newspapers.

In New York, Forcade had found a vehicle for his budding political paranoia: the anarchistic Yippies. He had been arrested for throwing pies at officials during a hearing of the Federal Commission on Obscenity and Pornography, and he had edited and prepared for publication Abbie Hoffman's *Steal This Book* when Yippie Number One was on the run. (At the time of the tour, he and Hoffman were continuing their long feud as to how much money Forcade is owed for the work; he still hasn't been paid.)

Forcade also wrote a book of his own, *Caravan of Love and Money,* which Warner Brothers foolishly tried to make into a film. Forcade felt it was his duty to do everything he could to disrupt the film. That's the funny part. The rumblings behind aren't funny. There are rumors that he is involved in drug and even gun smuggling. Everyone knows he has a violent streak.

During that time, Forcade acted as road manager for David Peel, an explicitly pro-pot rock musician (his first record was titled *Have a Marijuana;* his career deteriorated after he was unable to develop a second idea). Sometimes, to enhance Peel's show, Forcade would throw firecrackers onto the stage.

As Peel told *High Times*, "We had enough bodyguards to make the CIA and FBI envious. Tom Forcade made sure that everything was under control, and that nobody bothered us." Just like Monk is trying to do for the Sex Pistols.

In 1974, Forcade helped found *High Times*, a glossy magazine about drugs and the drug culture. The rise of Forcade and *High Times* paralleled (and helped shape) the explosion of the drug and drug-paraphernalia cultures in the mid- and late-seventies. As organizations like NORML (National Organization for the Reform of Marijuana Laws) came to relative power and prestige, so did Forcade. Within two years, *High Times* went from being published quarterly to being published monthly, circulation hovered over half a million, and by 1978 the magazine enjoyed an annual advertising base exceeding $1.5 million. *High Times*, with its articles about searching for the perfect bong hit and advertisements for the most esoteric of drug paraphernalia, became the focal point of the drug-tolerance and drug-legalization movements. *High Times* was the doper's monthly bible.

But with his success, the paranoia that pulled Forcade into politics in the mid-sixties turned on him. As soccer was beginning to gain a foothold in the United States, Forcade confided to Frank Fioramonti, a member of the NORML board of directors, that he was terrified that soccer stadiums in the United States would be used for political repression and torture, as they were in South America. He had his name removed from the masthead of the magazine he founded and hid because he was afraid government agents were following him. He frequently threatened magazine employees that he was shutting down *High Times* and firing everyone. Once he emphasized his threat by ripping telephone wires out of a receptionist's switchboard.

But paranoid as he has become, it is a twisted sense of idealism that brings Forcade to Memphis tonight. In the Sex Pistols, Forcade sees a last chance for genuine anarchy in the U.S.A., the dream he and his Yippie friends thrilled to a decade earlier over countless hash hits. Forcade was an early media supporter of punk. He put Deborah Harry on the cover of the June 1977 *High Times*, right next to the ALBERT GOLDMAN

EATS HASH and DOPE MANNERS: WERE YOU RAISED IN A BARN? teasers.

Forcade had been thrilled to put Johnny Rotten on the cover of *High Times* a few months later because he viewed this gingivitis-scarred demon as the voice of unsullied anger America needs so badly. He also loved the internal fight it took to get Rotten on his cover. The vast majority of the *High Times* staff considered the Grateful Dead the epitome of music and pop philosophy: They were appalled by the Sex Pistols. They were hippies and they wanted no association with this anti-hippie group. Most of the staff signed a petition to keep Johnny Rotten off the cover. Nobody thought it would sell. It turned out to be one of the best-selling *High Times* issues ever.

Forcade's politics are partially determined by his intense desire to go against the grain. In discussing Forcade's early years at *High Times,* friend and collaborator Russ Weiner told the publication, "Tom's political philosophy was: Whatever the predominant ideology, he was the opposite. Whatever you were for, he was against it and he just loved to be that way. . . . As soon as he thought you understood where he was at, he'd move to another place. Tom was a professional trouble-maker. Whenever there was chaos or people in turmoil, he was in his element."

It's no accident, then, that one of Forcade's favorite books is a science fiction work by Norman Spinrad, *Agent of Chaos.* As Weiner says, the novel "holds the idea that there is the right wing and the left wing, and then a third force. The right wing and the left wing are in this predictable dance together, but only the third force can move things forward. Tom liked to be that third force."

Forcade tells those close to him that he will use the tour to try to take over the Sex Pistols. He wants them to play at pot rallies. He wants to forge an alliance between whatever is left of the revolutionary marijuana movement and what he sees as the new revolutionary rock movement. Of course, he also wants to be the leader of these movements.

Forcade may believe in the Sex Pistols as envoys of Spinrad's third, idealistic wing, but he's still a formidable (if iconoclastic) businessman. He knows how to get what he wants.

The Sex Pistols have a fatal flaw—Vicious's increasingly public drug habit—and he's going to exploit it until he gets what he wants from Monk: complete access for his documentary. He's got Sid holed up in another room, waiting for his fix. He's got leverage.

"Calm down, Noel," Forcade instructs. "Sid came over about two hours ago looking for some smack. I think he's up with one of my photographers. Perhaps I can find him."

"Bullshit. Stop yanking my goddamn chain," Monk responds.

Forcade turns up the television volume to show his lack of respect; Monk turns it down. Forcade turns it back up again; the hotel security guard steps forward and turns off the set. Tempers flash; Monk and Forcade scream.

Seeing that he is accomplishing nothing this way, Monk asks the hotel security guard and D.W. to wait outside the room for a second.

Monk is familiar enough with Forcade's reputation to admit to himself that he doesn't have a clue as to what Forcade intends to do. He's also crazy enough from losing Sid twice in less than twenty-four hours not to worry about the ramifications of his actions.

"You motherfucker," Monk snarls, "I'm going to break your goddamn legs if you don't tell me where Sid is right now."

"Honest to God," Forcade says, suspecting that Monk's threat of violence is for real and making a mental note to hire his own bodyguards. "I don't know where he is. I think he's up on the third floor. He's up with a cameraman. I'm not sure. He could be up with a cameraman. They sent out for some smack for him. He's waiting for it. It may be here. I can check. He may be well. I can check. Can't we talk?"

"You lying sonofabitch," Monk fumes. "Where is Sid? I wanna know right now."

"Noel, I don't fucking know. I can find out, though, if we talk about this documentary. If we talk."

Monk walks to the door, opens it, and calls D.W. and the hotel security guard back into the room. The security guard turns the television up loud and D.W. locks the door behind them.

At that moment, a blood-curdling scream pierces the air, drowning out even the blasting television. Monk pulls the shade on Forcade's window to the side and gets a perfect view of Sid Vicious living up to his chosen name. Vicious stands at the side of the pool, with a sneer you could ski down, swinging his studded leather belt (another belt, a gift from Forcade an hour ago, lies on the grass) over his head. He's naked from the waist up, and the self-carving on his chest has clotted and inflamed to the point at which I WANNA FIX couldn't be more clear if it were spelled out in neon.

Monk, D.W., and the security man run out of Forcade's room toward the pool. In the hall, they pick up Boogie and yell at him to come with them.

Five feet away from Sid is one of the hotel's security men. His clothes are disheveled enough to make it clear that Vicious has kicked him around some. The security man reaches for his holster. He and Vicious are entirely absorbed in their fury at each other.

The security guard with Monk acts quickly and calmly. "Hey Joe, just calm down. Put your gun away. Get out of here." Joe shakes his head and himself back to coherence, curses at Sid, and steps back.

That tragedy averted, Monk, D.W., Boogie, and the other security guard all tackle Sid, who, at this point, becomes the strongest person any of them has ever encountered. Close to a minute of wild, furious maneuvering ensues.

"You can't fuckin' hold me down!" Vicious shouts. "Motherfuckers, let me up! Fuckin' let me up!"

They let him up, and the violence starts anew. Feet and fists fly. Monk takes a sharp kick in the ribs, Boogie takes a belt slash on the side of his face. Finally, D.W. takes control. Sid lunges at D.W., and the massive bodyguard grabs Sid and throws him over his shoulder. Sid lands on his back, flat. All fear that Sid will be out cold for hours, but after a few seconds he sits up. He's still ranting and raving, shouting, "Fuck all you guys! I'm not doin' anything! Stay away from me! Do the fuckin' show yourself! I gotta get some! I gotta get some." But for now, at least, he's just screaming. The violence has subsided. He's spent.

Monk and D.W. walk Sid into the hotel and prop him up

on the wall in a short corridor, next to a candy machine. Sid is in himself now, not communicating, but not hitting either. Off in the far corner of the hallway, Monk spies a skulking McLaren. With him is his assistant, Sophie Richmond, a slight, benign presence. (She won't be heard from again. She's with the band for the rest of the tour, but you'd never know it.)

"Sid," Monk beseeches, "Talk to D.W. for a little bit. Stay calm."

Monk walks to McLaren and tears into him. "It's your fucking act, Malcolm. Deal with him. You might not wanna go to the goddamn shows, but you're going to get your hands dirty right now. Understand?"

McLaren is offended by such a thought. "No, no. I can't do that. Haven't I explained myself already? He'll kill me. He hates me. He'll kill me."

Monk tries again. "Malcolm, it's your act. Deal with your artist."

"I'm sorry. I can't do it. That's not what I do."

"You little fucking wanker." Monk walks back to the slowly recovering Sid, with Malcolm all but cowering in a corner. McLaren isn't kidding. He is genuinely scared by this display of violence. He has encouraged a budding monster to become a full-grown one and now he can't control it anymore.

Monk tells Sid, "I know what you want. You're not getting it."

Sid's anger has turned poignant. He's overtired and going through cold turkey, looking for some hope.

Vicious leans against Monk and says, "Mate, I'm bloody gone. Is there any possible way you can get me some heroin? Tom said he could."

"No. No fucking way."

"Then is there any way you can get me some methadone? I need it bad, mate, bad. Any way? Any bloody way?"

"I'll try, Sid. I promise I'll try. But you have to do the show. Your mates are waiting."

"But I need a fix."

"Listen, I said I'd try," Monk's temper returns. "So, whatcha gonna do, Sid? You can ruin the whole fucking show, the whole fucking tour. You can also let your mates down. They're sitting in the lobby waiting to go to the show. They've been sitting out there for half an hour. What are you gonna do about them? What are you gonna tell them?"

Monk cuts through Vicious's junkie haze with word that his behavior is hurting his three comrades, and Sid begins to talk rationally about doing the show. Monk helps soothe him, helps to talk Vicious in off the ledge the poor kid has built for himself.

After about five minutes of this, Sid is ready to play. "All right, all right, all right. Let's do it. Let's fuckin' rock! Where's my bass?"

Rotten, Jones, and Cook are furious with Vicious when D.W. walks him into the lobby.

"Oh, look," Rotten hisses. "Here comes Mister Drug. Hello, Mister Drug. Thinking about perhaps showing up for the performance tonight, Sid-nay?"

Vicious ignores Rotten and walks toward the bus between Jones and Cook. "Hello, sidemen," he says. "How does it feel to be part of the backing band?"

Rotten, Jones, and Cook avoid all contact with Vicious. They walk to the bus in silence. It is starting to snow.

11 P.M.

No one else in the band answers Sid when he speaks to them. They're growing tired of his antics; they want a real bass player, although probably not Paul McCartney.

Outside the Taliesyn Ballroom, Cohen's earlier warning of an impending riot isn't far off the mark. Promoter Bob Kelly, owner of Mid-South Productions, was made to understand that the capacity of the Taliesyn Ballroom, a hall he doesn't normally book, is twelve hundred. He sold all twelve hundred tickets. The only problem is that the Fire Marshal's limit for the Taliesyn Ballroom is actually seven hundred twenty-five, and there are five hundred angry ticket holders being told they can't get in. The Fire Marshals have failed to disperse them, as have normal police forces. After the outsiders start throwing cans through the front windows of the hall, the police call the SWAT force. Vicious enters the hall swigging vodka.

Like Monk, Johnston does not want Forcade's film crew at the gig, but he inadvertently lets Mickey Rabbit into the club along with the slew of press photographers.

They are only an hour and a half late. The Warner Brothers people are going out of their minds; the promoter is suicidal, and the police want their heads. The usual.

There's a double irony to the band's being unwelcome in Memphis. Memphis is the cradle of rock and roll, the environment that spawned the purest, most potent rock and roll of all. Sun Records, the first label of rock and roll, came out of Memphis. Elvis Presley got his start here. So did Jerry Lee Lewis, Carl Perkins, Roy Orbison, Charlie Rich, and Johnny Cash. Memphis is the unquestioned capital of rock and roll (and soul, thanks to the grand achievements of Stax Records, which defined soul in the sixties). There's little in rock and roll even as late as 1978 that doesn't refer back to Sun in some way.

But Memphis doesn't want the Sex Pistols to soil its pristine reputation. Although the music that came out of Sam Phillips's Sun Studio in the mid- and late-fifties remains among rock and roll's wildest, the music Phillips fostered turned into rock-and-roll establishment. For all the unquenched energy that he started with, Elvis did end up playing Las Vegas. And as far as the polite establishment is concerned, the Sex Pistols can go to hell.

Not everyone in the Old Guard feels that way. Rock founding father Carl Perkins notes that the Sex Pistols are another link in the unending chain of rock-and-roll tradition. He tells John Morthland in *Rolling Stone,* "The Sex Pistols' music is almost like some of the fifties-style stuff, it's so simple. I didn't understand what they mean by sticking pins through their noses, but they never cover up that basic thing, which is the beat that makes kids tap their feet or get up on the dance floor."

Or scrawl I WANNA FIX across their chests, for that matter. More than twenty years after Elvis rocked the world awake, even the iconoclasts recall Sun's simplicity and determination. As much as Rotten and McLaren want their band to be the one that cuts rock and roll (or rock, as it is now more pretentiously termed) in two, the Sex Pistols are part of the tradition, whether they like it or not.

Jim Dickinson, one of the lucky ticket holders who has been allowed into the Taliesyn Ballroom, recognizes this. Dickinson is an old-timer on the Memphis rock scene—he's been around long enough to have been associated with the later days of Sun Records as leader of the Jesters, recorded with many of the city's first line of bluesmen, and played piano on the Rolling Stones' 1971 hit "Wild Horses." He's fascinated by the Sex Pistols, enough so to brave the crowd and the snow. He's friends with Carl Scott and fellow Warner Brothers executive Jo Bergman, the label's director of special projects. (Dickinson's friendship with Bergman reaches back to the time when they were both associated with the Rolling Stones.)

"There was a certain repulsive quality to rock in the fifties that didn't come back until the Sex Pistols," Dickinson says. "They are such a vicious assault on the audience, something that is traditionally supposed to be a part of rock and roll."

Dickinson, who has entered through a side door, sees the Sex Pistols walk out with the house lights on. Someone has thrown a sport coat onto Sid. Vicious looks nearly presentable; he isn't exuding what Dickinson calls his "Frankenstein-half-naked-drinking-blood look."

The band poses to play, and on the first note the lights drop down. The lights flash back. Sid's jacket is gone, his T-shirt is ripped to the point of being useless except as an accessory, and everyone in the crowd can see how bloody he has made his chest. The sound is abominable, an impenetrable wall of solid mud (thank you, Boogie), far less distinct than that at the Great South East. The lyrics are a blur. What jumps from Rotten's microphone is all snarl and destruction.

"I'm not here for your amusement," Rotten barks at the audience after the first song. "You're here for mine. Now stop throwing things at me!"

The strain that Vicious's addiction has inflicted on the band is evident on the stage. Cook and Jones are playing harder and faster—more brutally—than they did last night in Atlanta. They're all furious, and they're taking it out on the music.

Many of the curious are here tonight to see one of Vicious's gross-outs, but the frantic Rotten cedes top billing to no one tonight. He's more animated and lively than he was in Atlanta. He dances around the stage and points at the audience to implicate them in his evil thoughts. He stands at the edge of the stage and leans the top half of his body over the crowd, like a skyscraper jumper gathering his final thoughts.

As a musician, Dickinson is transfixed by Steve Jones's guitar sound. Jones positions two small Fender amplifiers on chairs next to each other. One of the amps is plugged into the other, with the vibrato turned way up on both of them. He points one amp at the other, so that the notes sound twice as fast as they actually are. It speeds up the locomotive that is the Sex Pistols into a ringing, raging runaway.

Also in the hall is John Holmstrom, editor of *Punk* magazine, who's there at the last-minute invitation of Forcade. Forcade distributes *Punk* as part of his alternative magazine distribution service (he also funds the magazine on the sly), and he recognizes the importance of the Sex Pistols tour to *Punk*'s audience. If Johnny Rotten on the cover of *High Times* is a sellout, imagine how many copies of *Punk* the boy's scowl could sell!

Holmstrom got a call this morning at his New York office from Forcade. "Come on down to Memphis," Forcade said. "We'll take care of you."

When he gets to Memphis, Holmstrom spends his last twenty dollars on a cab to the Taliesyn Ballroom. He has no money, no ticket. Luckily, Gary Kenton, a Warner Brothers publicist, recognizes him and lets him in. Holmstrom will be following the Sex Pistols for the remainder of the tour, both as a reporter for *Punk* and an agent for Forcade. He loves the show. So far, it's worth the aggravation.

Toward the end of the show, the side door flies open, and in rushes the SWAT team. They've successfully dispersed the crowd outside (with help from the snow), and have decided to make a typical Memphis antirock statement. They look around and quickly leave. It is well past the time when anything bad could have happened, but they want to remind everyone who's in charge.

2 A.M.

In the darkened parking lot of the Holiday Inn, while the band members and crew pack and prepare for an all-night drive to Texas, Monk meets with two Warner Brothers executives. They know that Sid has a problem—no one, not even a record-company executive, is that blind—but until now they didn't have an inkling of its severity.

"This kid has a bad problem," Monk says. "I've got to get him something. Right now he's living on alcohol and my Valium. That's getting him by, but the boy is hurting. He can't sleep, he doesn't hold any food down."

Monk hasn't had a good day himself: After the show, as he walked Sid upstairs to a dressing room, he got so angry at Forcade that he punched out a window. If nothing else, the act impressed Vicious. The executives say they'll do what they can, but Monk is seasoned enough as a tour manager to know when a record company doesn't want to address a problem.

Monk returns to the hotel and gives Sid the bad news. "I tried, like I said I would, but it doesn't look like we're getting any. They won't get methadone."

"Then could you get me some smack?"

"No way."

Sid's face turns even more pallid. "Then could you get me my Valiums? I need my Valiums."

"No problem."

Pallid and maudlin. "And could you stay up and talk with me when I have to stay up? I love to talk with you, Monk. Bloody hell."

"No problem," Monk says. "If you have a problem, let's talk. That's why we're rooming together. That's why we have walkie-talkies. Now get your stuff. We have a bus to catch. We're going to Texas."

CHAPTER SEVEN

Day Five: Saturday, January 7—Austin

Noon

THE ALL-NIGHT DRIVE from Memphis is almost finished, but the bus isn't taking the Sex Pistols to a San Antonio hotel in advance of Sunday night's concert, as was originally planned.

Monk and Johnston have been alerted by both Warner Brothers and members of the tour entourage to the death threats that await the Sex Pistols in San Antonio. "Come on down to our town you fucking godless limeys," one of the notes allegedly reads. "We'll rip out your fucking lungs and make you wish you'd never left your own fucking country."

Whether the threats are genuine or manufactured by McLaren doesn't matter. The crew decides to treat them as if they are real and spend as little time as possible in San Antonio.

"The rednecks want to kill all of us," Johnston tells Monk as they board the bus. "We should get more bodyguards like the Chinese muscle men Forcade just picked up." Johnston is convinced that the Sex Pistols are about to enter hostile, alien territory.

"I know, I know." As the bus leaves Memphis and crosses the Mississippi River into Arkansas, Monk picks up a road map and looks for an alternative to San Antonio. He sees that Austin, the capital of Texas, is less than ninety miles north of San Antonio. He instructs Charles, the band's new bus driver, to take them only as far as Austin. Austin is close enough to San Antonio to make a quick run south the afternoon of the show; it's also far enough that Monk and Johnston will feel safe. Austin is a government city, a college town, nothing like San Antonio.

In addition to a new bus driver for the remainder of the tour, the Sex Pistols also have a new bus. In Memphis the only bus Monk could find to rent for a day was a slightly refurbished city bus, but for the rest of the journey the band has a bona fide rock-star tour bus. There are six sleeping bunks, three on each side (right now, they're all full), and room to stretch out in back.

After the escalating tension in Atlanta and Memphis, this all-night ride is a release for the band and crew. Those in the know are worried about what might be waiting for them in San Antonio, but on the bus no one can do any damage and there is no way Sid can get away.

Yet Vicious is the only member of the band who has been awake for the majority of the ride. He sits in the bus's shotgun seat, exchanging banalities with Charles and staring out the front window. As Charles negotiates the bus diagonally down and across Arkansas via I-40 and I-30, there's not much for Sid to see. It's dark outside, the roads are mostly deserted, and the lights and truckstops on the side of the interstates are minimal. It takes Charles just under five hours to get the band through Arkansas and into Texas.

As the bus passes through Texarkana in the pre-dawn hours and crosses the Texas state line, Charles breathes a sigh of relief.

"Texas!" Vicious coughs as they enter the state. "I gotta get a cowboy hat like Steve's. We're in Texas."

No ambush is waiting for the band at the border, as had been rumored, even though the bus is an easy target: Fans in Memphis have spray-painted the bus with band slogans. The Sex Pistols are in the middle of nowhere. The nearest semi-city, Mount Pleasant, is an hour away. By the time the bus reaches the liquor-dry metropolis of Mount Pleasant, even Vicious has nodded out. He slumps in his seat, cradling an empty bottle of vodka.

As the bus passengers start to awake around noon,

Charles has driven them through Dallas and Waco, and they're less than two hours outside of Austin. Before Sid has a chance to wake up and cause trouble on a stop, Charles pulls over to a rest area and gives Monk an opportunity to book rooms at the Austin Ramada Inn. As the bus returns to highway speed, Vicious begins to rejoin the world of the semiconscious.

The only significant member of the entourage who is missing is McLaren. Unwilling to spend the night in a tour bus, he has stayed behind in Memphis and will fly American to San Antonio later in the afternoon. He will fly first class.

The American crew notices that Vicious needs a bath. The groggy band members are used to Sid's lack of hygiene and don't notice anymore. It's not that Rotten, Jones, or Cook are particularly well-kempt; it's just that the scent around the bass player is more distinctive by the hour.

The four smelly band members are anxious to see America. They have a romantic vision of everything in America, and McLaren has ingrained in them the belief that Texas is the "real America." They all are peering out the windows, taking in the roadside ranches and tacky signs with plastic longhorns atop them. They flood the American crew with banal questions about America. For now, the Sex Pistols are inquisitive tourists.

Rotten looks up from a road map. "We passed Dallas," he informs. "I thought we were going to Dallas."

"We're going to Dallas, all right," Charles says from the driver's seat. "But not for a couple of days. We're heading south to San Antonio, east to Baton Rouge, then back up to Dallas. We'll be getting there on Tuesday."

"Tuesday?" Rotten asks. "When's bloody Tuesday? I can't even remember what day it is anymore. What? It's Saturday? Well, welcome to the weekend. It's Saturday Night Fever time. Shall we boogie down, then?"

As the miles roll on, inhibitions fade and wariness disappears. An unspoken sentiment of "we're all in this together" arises. No one in the band tries to defy authority, because for once no one in the crew needs to exert authority.

Rotten asks questions about the Ramones: Are they big here? Will we get a chance to meet them? Johnny is interested in the Ramones, but he's not curious about the rock industry as a whole. He doesn't respect it. But the Ramones are the great American punk band, kindred spirits and competition.

The Sex Pistols are different from the Ramones in every respect. The Ramones' public image is of dumb cartoon-character hoods. They even let cartoon drawings of them replace photographs on their album covers and promotional materials. The Ramones' idea of how to get punk to the masses is by turning it into a joke. But after the initial rush, people don't want to read about a joke—if you want to sustain something, you have to give them the real thing.

Monk notices that this small group is garnering more press attention than he's seen on any tour, and the Ramones are getting nothing. He's overseen many tours with major acts from the Moody Blues to the Rolling Stones, but this is unprecedented. It's because of the media attention that he realizes that this phenomenon is shaking up the music business.

Everyone except for Charles is drinking. Some partake in the occasional joint; all are relaxed. The appearance of pot inspires Sid to pop a cassette, the only one he has brought with him from England, into the bus's sound system. Reggae's shanking rhythms ooze through the bus, lulling all into complacency. Even Noel is relaxed.

"You like this shit?" someone in the road crew asks the band.

"Reggae is real," Rotten retorts. "It doesn't come out of some phony London studio. Or a phony, expensive, disgusting New York studio, I might add."

"Thanks for the explanation, Johnny boy."

It makes sense that the punk rockers of London in general and the Sex Pistols in particular would be attracted to the reggae of performers like Bob Marley, Toots Hibbert, and Jimmy Cliff. The Clash's amazing debut LP (the import version of which is reaching these shores in record numbers because the American arm of CBS deems it "too crude for release") strays from its breakneck pace only once, for a devastating cover of the dark, defiant Junior Marvin reggae tune "Police and Thieves." The subject matter isn't all that different: anarchy, police and thieves.

Reggae is rebel music, socially conscious music, and, not

incidentally, music to get stoned by. The cult of Rastafari, to which many prominent Jamaican reggae musicians subscribe, states that ganja is a sacrament. The scent of the sacrament quickly fills the tour bus.

Everyone in the Sex Pistols has thrilled to the reggae cult film *The Harder They Come,* which starred singer Cliff as a violent gangster, a trenchtown Stagger Lee. In the film's title track Cliff sings, "I'll keep on fighting for the things I want/Though I know that when you're dead you can't/But I'd rather be a free man in my grave/Than living as a puppet or a slave/So as sure as the sun will shine/I'm gonna get my share now, what's mine/And then the harder they come/The harder they fall/One and all."

Just as punk is the music of London's poor whites, reggae is an escape from poverty for many of Kingston's poor blacks. The only other option many see is crime. In *The Harder They Come,* Cliff lives up to both myths (or stereotypes, if you like). He's a pop star as much for his six-shooter as his six-string. Cliff is a bad-ass in the film; the band members want to be bad-asses, too. Their music doesn't have the rhythm of reggae, but punk and reggae share the same defiant attitude.

As the bus continues south through Texas, the band members remain fascinated by the countryside, asking hundreds of questions about America, taking it all in. Sid's tape blurts out the lusty dubs of the leading exponents of dub, a type of reggae in which deejays rap over a backing track. On the tape, performers such as U. Roy, I. Roy, and Big Youth declaim in patois about everything from social injustice to their sexual prowess. Dub is the most democratic form of reggae: All one needs to make a workable dub recording is a healthy dose of audacity.

The tape playing is *Version Galore, Volume Three,* a compilation record taking in dub music recorded between 1971 to 1973 on Trojan Records, the prime British disseminator of Jamaican reggae. I. Roy's "Space Flight" and Big Youth's "Foreman vs. Frazier" are top-rank dub. They're witty, far-ranging raps set atop alternately silky and ominous rhythms. Padding out the tape are a few more recent tracks by less impressive performers. Sid may feel an affinity to reggae, but he isn't particularly discerning.

The band members are still fatigued, but they are so fascinated by Texas that they can't turn away. Even as they play cards, they repeatedly look out the window.

With the marijuana no doubt playing a role, the Sex Pistols begin to open up to their American hosts or protectors or jailers. The Americans talk of America; the Sex Pistols talk of their exploits.

"We got into the biggest fuckin' fights on the Continent," Jones says. "It would have been keen to have a geezer like D.W. on our side there."

"There's so much you've taken for granted about our doings that are not at all true," Rotten says. "The filthy British press—if you can call them that—exaggerate what they've heard about and add to it. They're adding lies to lies to lies. It's bloody awful, I say."

All have forgotten for now the San Antonio threats. All are relaxed. Cook and Jones play poker with the crew and trade jokes. Jones looks for a way to cheat.

Sid seems especially relaxed after his brief sleep. He's popping Valium—Monk has a prescription that he intends to refill for Vicious every chance he can—and that seems to help ease the heroin withdrawal. He inhales a few pills, and he washes them down with peppermint schnapps.

Monk sits down next to Vicious. "Are you enjoying the Valium?"

"Yeah, yeah. I'm having a great time in America, Monk. Bloody well mean it. I'm happy."

"I'm glad to hear that."

"Hey, do you want to see what I do when I'm happy?"

Sid pulls a knife out of his pocket (who let him on the bus with a knife?) and opens a deep seven-inch gap on his left arm. The blood pours, then spurts. Blood splashes the seats, the windows, the walls.

Yet Vicious doesn't seem hurt. Rather he's bemused, like a kid who's made a mess and wants the added pleasure of watching someone else clean it.

"Sid, that's going to be a lot of fun to work with," Monk shrugs and starts to clean. He knows not to act shocked. That only encourages Vicious.

Rotten sneers at Vicious. "Oh no, boys. Not again. Our

friend with the drugs has cut himself. Bollocks, Sidney, don't you ever learn? Don't you ever fuckin' learn?"

Soon Sid's arm stops pouring blood. A crew member walks Vicious to the bathroom in the back of the bus to continue cleaning his arm. Coupled with the chemical smell of the bus bathroom, the scent around Vicious isn't particularly enticing.

Good morning.

2 P.M.

Forcade and Holmstrom pace the halls of their San Antonio hotel, looking for Sex Pistols. They have the official itinerary. This is where the band is supposed to stay. Where are they?

By now, Forcade has assembled his own entourage. Between the *Punk* contingent and his film crew, he has more people on the Sex Pistols tour than Warner Brothers. But the tour is frustrating for Forcade. The club owners don't want movie cameras in their clubs. The Sex Pistols don't want movie cameras in the clubs. Yet there are many around the Sex Pistols who like Forcade realize the importance of having the movie made, so the film crew is often able to get their sound right out of the sound board. There are constantly people letting them in, people kicking them out, people letting them back in. It's hard work.

Yet Forcade's problems are more with his own company than with the Sex Pistols and Warner Brothers. Forcade is spending a fortune of his company's money on this film, and those in his company who don't like the idea of a Sex Pistols movie financed by *High Times* are beginning to balk at the flights from city to city and the rented limousines. Forcade uses company credit cards to avoid having to deal with the home office.

Forcade wants his Sex Pistols movie to be an outlaw movie, so on one hand he doesn't mind that he doesn't have official sanction by Warner Brothers. On the other hand, the paranoid Forcade is afraid Warner Brothers will have him beat up in an attempt to avoid another debacle like *Caravan of Love and Money.* So Forcade has hired his own bodyguards.

4 P.M.

Thornton Arnold, the bell captain at the Ramada Inn of Austin, has never seen anything like the Sex Pistols before. They can stay in the hotel, but they'd better stay off to the side, away from the guests. Just in case.

Rotten tells Allison, "This hotel is bloody awful. Let's take a walk. I want to see this city." They walk for two blocks, where they reach a movie theater. They see *The Gauntlet,* the latest Clint Eastwood-Sondra Locke police thriller. So much for seeing the city.

Monk and Vicious have adjoining rooms at the Ramada Inn. The other band members are downstairs in the hotel bar insulting the bartender, but Monk won't let his bass player out of his sight. Monk inspects Sid's arm. He doesn't like what he sees.

"Sid, this is getting infected."

"So?"

"That's not good."

"Whaddya mean, Monk?"

"I mean it's not good. It could get worse. It could puff up more."

"Am I going to die from this?"

"Die? No, you're not going to die. You're . . ." At that moment, Monk flashes back to Rotten's reaction to the lightning scare during the flight to Memphis and realizes that however much the Sex Pistols talk about death and destruction, they have a respect for life, at least their own. ". . . you're gonna be fine, Sid."

"Good, good."

"But to make it better, I'm gonna do something that might hurt a bit. Is that OK?"

Sid comes alive. "Yeah, Monk. Make it hurt. Make it fucking hurt."

Monk pours a bottle of Mercurochrome on Vicious's arm, and his patient screams.

"Sid, this is pain. This is what you wanted. You're supposed to like it."

"Man, this motherfucker hurts!"

"Yeah, that's the idea." Monk washes it out with peroxide and bandages Vicious.

"I wanna go out."

"You can't go out."

"Why not?"

"Because I fucking said so. You hurt yourself something awful."

"I wanna go out."

"I said you can't go out."

"I'm goin' out."

"You're not goin' anywhere."

Sid is getting agitated. The last time Sid was agitated, Monk needed three other people to help him get Sid under control.

"All right," Monk says. "You win. We'll go out. Let's take a walk together."

Sid walks out of the hotel leaning forward, cruising on Valium and peppermint schnapps. As he walks out of the hotel, he waves at passers-by. He should have been out earlier. He could use the sun. He looks like a ghost; he's Casper the Friendly Punk.

The violence Sid had shown in Memphis disappears completely. He is a pleasure to be with. Of course, this doesn't stop Monk from continuing to beg him to take a bath.

The Ramada Inn is in downtown Austin, near the University of Texas campus and the state capitol complex. The students and politicians that pass by the slow-walking pair of Vicious and Monk are for the most clean-cut. Vicious stands out. He waves at people. Some notice him and wave back; most walk past.

"This is fucking great," Sid exults. "These are people! I'm talking to the people!"

Vicious and Monk are only a block or two away from being in the shadow of a landmark that the Sex Pistols might identify with more easily than a state capitol.

A few blocks away is the University of Texas's notorious 231-foot clock tower. On August 1, 1966, the day after he killed his wife and mother, an ex-Marine sharpshooter named Charles Whitman stood on the tower's observation deck and fired down indiscriminately for ninety terrifying minutes. By the time he was shot and killed by an Austin police officer, Whitman had shot forty-five people from the tower. Fourteen of them died from their wounds.

"It'll happen to you," the tower's security guard told reporters afterwards.

To the Sex Pistols, Whitman would be a Stagger Lee, a Jimmy Cliff, an icon.

For once on this tour, a Sex Pistol is far away from any such inklings of violence. Vicious is comfortable, loaded, friendly, imperturbable. What's in a name?

Monk and Vicious walk in wide circles around the capitol area. During their marathon walk, Sid brings up many subjects he hadn't yet broached, most notably Nancy Spungen, his girlfriend.

Spungen is an underage Philadelphia-born groupie/ junkie who journeyed to London in 1976 with then-boyfriend and fellow junkie Johnny Thunders, once a member of the New York Dolls and now the leader of his own clearly ill-fated band, the Heartbreakers. McLaren, who is often at odds with Spungen over what's "best" for Sid—as if either of them really care—must get wry satisfaction over the fact that Sid's girlfriend comes to him after being dumped by a member of a band McLaren once semimanaged, the Dolls.

After Thunders dumped Spungen, young Nancy latched onto Vicious and introduced him to hard drugs and hard love. The rest of the band, particularly Rotten, hate Nancy. In one unfortunate package she is everything the Sex Pistols ostensibly rail against: a loud, hippie American with pretensions. But Sid, in his strangely innocent way, has fallen in love with the belligerent bleached blonde. Their passion frequently explodes into violence—what else could be expected? When he left for America for who knew how long, leaving Nancy in London to feed her habit by turning tricks with her lesbian prostitute friend Linda, he was deeply troubled, if only for a day.

But this isn't what Sid is talking about. He's got a more pressing need.

"I need money, Monk."

"For what?"

"No, not smack money. Money for Nancy."

"I thought you said Nancy was making a good living in London."

"Yeah, yeah. She is. But I've got to save enough money so I can fly Nancy back to America."

"Your visa expires in a few weeks. You'll be back in London soon enough."

"No, no. I have to get her to America. I have to get her to a plastic surgeon."

"I thought you said she was beautiful."

"She is beautiful, Monk. But I have to get her to a plastic surgeon to get the birthmark off her arse so she can become a stripper."

"You want her to become a stripper."

"She wants to be a stripper."

"What do you want?"

"I want her to be a stripper. She'd be a great stripper. It's the right thing for her to do."

The pair conclude their walk to the state capitol steps. They pass statues commemorating the southern side of the Civil War. None of the plaques accompanying the statues suggests that preservation of slavery, the cause of the South in that conflict, was anything less than righteous.

Sid and Noel sit down, share what's left of Sid's second bottle of peppermint schnapps, and rap. It's a beautiful evening.

CHAPTER EIGHT

Day Six: Sunday, January 8—San Antonio

6 P.M.

THE BAND HAS CELEBRATED Elvis's first birthday six feet under by sleeping most of the day. Midafternoon, all pile into the bus for the quick run down to San Antonio. "Burning Love," Presley's last great hit, plays from the bus radio as the band members file in. They ape Presley's "Hun-ka hun-ka burnin' love" chorus.

Vicious decides to ride shotgun. "How ya doin'?" he asks Charles as the bus pulls out of the parking lot.

"Fine, fine," Charles says. "Not much of a drive today. We just goin' two hours to San Anton."

"All right then," Vicious says. "You'll need the rest. You're gonna be our second guitar player tonight."

"Yeah, right," Charles chuckles. "I'll get the razor blades put in my cheek when we get there."

For the first time on the tour, the Sex Pistols can enjoy taking in the sights while fully awake. Unfortunately, there's not much to see during this relatively brief drive. The landmark that attracts the most attention is the Snake Farm just south of Austin.

"Do they grow snakes there?" Jones asks.

No one responds; all are afraid that Jones's question may be in earnest. Locals rumor that the Snake Farm is actually a front for a whorehouse.

Vicious and Monk stare out the front window from their shotgun seats.

"I'm worried," Sid says after he downs another mouthful of peppermint schnapps.

"What's up?" Monk asks.

"There's something wrong with me. I know it. I fucked some bird before I got here and I fucking itch like crazy, mate. I think I have some bad disease."

"What else is wrong?"

"What else? Nothing. I fucking can't stop itching." Sid scratches hard as he talks.

Monk doesn't blink. "Sid, if that's all you've got, you've got nothing to worry about. You've got crabs, that's all."

"That's it?"

"That's it."

"If that's all it is, then fuck it."

The talk of venereal disease has distracted Vicious from his usual obsession: heroin. Now all he wants to talk about is sex.

"I miss fuckin' Nancy. I miss it a fuckin' lot. I gotta get some girls out here."

"So get some girls, as long as they're not from Warner Brothers."

"Yeah, I remember," Vicious says. "But you won't let me into the crowd. How can I stuff a bird if you won't let me into the crowd? It's impossible."

"No problem," Monk says. "Next show, I'll take care of that. Point 'em out and I'll bring 'em to you. I promise. And one other thing: Would you please take a fucking shower?"

Monk walks toward the back of the bus and antes into the security crew's poker game. In the center of the table is a pet rock.

"This has got to be the stupidest thing I've seen in my entire life," Allison says, pointing to the rock. "A pet rock. What a fucking waste."

"What'll they think of next?" Red asks.

"Vicious crabs," D.W. volunteers. "Did you hear Sid up there with his crabs? Unless he starts bathing in A-200, by the end of the tour we'll have enough of the damn things to open franchises."

7 P.M.

Back at their hotel, Forcade and Holmstrom resign themselves to the band's disappearance.

Holmstrom is still unhappy with the treatment he got at the hands of the Sex Pistols' security crew in Memphis Friday night. Because Holmstrom is associated with Forcade, the crew has instructions to keep him away. Holmstrom is there to cover the tour as a reporter, but his association with Forcade taints him in the mind of the crew. "There's no need to treat people as shabbily as Noel does," he tells Forcade. "He could have been professional about it, but at every point he was trying to keep us away from the story. He never gave us a break. He's a total creep. He doesn't understand the Sex Pistols. He doesn't understand what's going on."

Meeting Forcade and Holmstrom at the hotel is Roberta Bayley, a photographer for *Punk* magazine that Forcade has flown in from New York. Bayley is the definitive New York punk photographer. She has worked for CBGB, and she shot the cover of the first Ramones album.

Back on Friday, Bayley had felt left out when Holmstrom got the call from Forcade, but yesterday it was her turn to fly to points unknown. Holmstrom called her and told her she could have a one-way ticket to San Antonio. As far as she knows, she is just going for this one show. Holmstrom was extremely secretive on the phone this morning; she has no idea who is sending her to Texas. Last night, she went to see the Ramones at the Palladium, then packed. This morning, she was on the plane to Texas. Sitting behind her in first class on the plane was *Rolling Stone* photographer Annie Leibovitz, who's also flying to San Antonio to cover the show.

Although Bayley had made it to San Antonio, Holstrom and Forcade are still very secretive.

"We have to find the band," Holmstrom tells her. Forcade suggests they stake out different hotels.

Forcade and Holmstrom are wearing well-tailored western outfits that Forcade bought for them (on a company credit card) when Holmstrom met him in Memphis. Forcade is into costumes and dressing in a role. He also believes such attire will make it easier for them to rent rooms in good hotels than if they wear hippie or punk attire. Forcade doesn't have much money with him, and he wants it to look as if he and his entourage have money.

At Randy's Rodeo, the crew sets up the stage for a perfunctory sound check.

"Tom Forcade is CIA," McLaren says to Johnston, standing at the side of the stage. "The CIA is after us."

"You're kidding."

Rumors alleging that Forcade was an FBI agent date back to the 1972 Democratic convention in Miami. The myth was fabricated by narcotic agents seeking to discredit his reputation. In the counterculture, there's no quicker way to destroy someone's reputation than to call him a cop.

Johnston passes the word on to Monk. "Keep these fucking people away," he says. "Forcade's people are dangerous."

"Sure," Monk says. "It'll be my pleasure."

McLaren and Johnston hypothesize that Forcade and his entourage are plants from "some John-Birch-Society type of organization," as Johnston puts it. "Maybe they're here to help create and cause trouble."

McLaren loves the idea. Johnston, who's more interested in getting through the tour without any band members dying, is less enchanted.

10 P.M.

Just before the show, Holmstrom conducts an interview with McLaren. A few minutes into the disinformation dissemination, Cook and Jones charge into the room. They quickly right themselves, like children who didn't know they were barging in on adults.

"Steve and me are supposed to be doing an interview with the *Los Angeles Times*," Cook tells McLaren.

"Well, why aren't you there, then?" quizzes McLaren.

"I said 'fuck you' a few times and left," Cook responds and giggles.

"Good," McLaren says. "That's lovely. That's exactly what they want to hear, all right."

Jones wants some attention, too. "I told him to fuck off and I fuckin' farted in his face."

"Charming," McLaren offers.

"And I'm hungry," Jones says.

"So why don't you get something to eat, Steven?" McLaren asks. "There are some charming deli platters backstage."

"All right, then." Jones and Cook scamper out.

"I hear it's mostly working-class Mexicans buying tickets for the show," McLaren says, returning to the interview.

"Mexicans?" Holmstrom asks. "There'll probably be violence."

"That's what we're hoping for, yes." McLaren strokes his chin to appear thoughtful. He speaks slowly so Holmstrom gets everything down. "We wanted to play the deep South but Warner Brothers wouldn't let us."

"You want to play places like Mississippi and Alabama? It's horrible down there."

"Yes, yes," McLaren acknowledges. "We want to see how horrible it is. We want to see real cowboys, not just the rhinestone imitations."

McLaren's wish is about to come true.

Midnight

Randy's Rodeo is an old bowling alley, and the stage is stretched across the area where the lanes once ended. It's the first night of the tour when the weather outside is hot. The air conditioning inside is useless against a hall full of smoke, beer bottles, and sweat, and a dusty floor.

Under the bright white, orange, and blue house lights, the band asks for no quarter and concedes less. Cook beats his drums into compliance, Jones leaps into each power chord with a vengeance, Vicious tosses his pus-soaked bandage into the anxious crowd. His self-destruction has become an integral part of the show. It's what's expected of him and he's happy to live up to it.

Rotten, tucked into the brand-new black-leather pants

and cowboy vest he bought in Austin with Allison, screeches his most evil ideas like an apocalyptic banshee. "Screaming bloody mess!" he bays over and over during "Bodies." The music washes over the crowd, forcing them into submission, pulling them back in on the undertow.

The security crew stands on the front and sides of the stage. By now, Monk has started wearing a baseball hat to the shows, so he doesn't get spit on his head. The jackets and ties with which he started the tour are long gone.

It appears as if the Randy's Rodeo show is even more oversold than the Taliesyn Ballroom gig two nights ago. The place is beyond packed. Unlike the previous show, the hot, sweat-and-beer-drenched air here is filled with confrontation. It's not just paper cups that are being thrown at the band members tonight. Ripped-in-two beer cans, broken bottles, and mustard-drenched hot dogs zoom past for the entire seventy-minute show. Many in the audience mean to do harm (it's no accident that the following morning's paper refers to the show as a "shoot-out"). The insults being thrown at the stage drown out Rotten's between-song patter.

"All you cowboys are fuckin' faggots," Rotten taunts above the shouting. "You're all sorry cunts. And we don't like your fuckin' free gifts."

Vicious walks next to Rotten. "It's just like Iggy said," he says, leaning into the center microphone. "You're the fuckers who paid ten bucks to see us, so fuck you."

"Shut up, Sidney," Rotten says, and pulls back the microphone stand. "You're holding up the set." Then he turns his anger back at the crowd. "Go ahead! Throw all the cans you want! It amuses us to watch fools throw their money away! Throw all yer fuckin' money!"

In the back of the hall, a group of Mexican kids and cowboy kids are fighting. The confrontations tonight aren't limited to the group.

The British photographers also turn nasty tonight. Because of Rotten's instructions to keep the homeland press away, the security crew won't let any photographers near the band, near the stage, unless they are Americans. Tempers flare; photographers are routinely ejected. Forcade's crew has company in the parking lot.

One person weaving his way to the front of the crowd certainly means no good. "Let me at 'em!" he screams as he pushes pogoing punks aside and stands before the low stage. He shoves those who try to regain their places.

He stands up front against the stage, taunting the band members to come at him. "You wanna fuckin' fight? You wanna get nuts?" he yells at Rotten. "I'll show you a fight!"

Rotten ignores him, so the heckler moves to his left and starts taunting Vicious. When Vicious stands near the lip of the stage, the man in the crowd leans forward, waiting for his chance to take a swipe. More full beer cans head toward the stage. One grazes Vicious's side and annoys him. He staggers back a step and holds his side.

"Can't you take a fucking beer can, you limey baby?" the man up front screams. Sid has had enough. Although he's supposed to be playing a song, he takes his bass off his chest and holds it over his head. He walks to the front of the stage and sends the body of his bass into the crowd. The security crew pulls Sid away from the edge of the stage, but not until he has sent his bass crashing down twice. The rest of the band continues to play. They don't mind the missing bass.

Sid is too drunk to notice, but he hasn't done much damage to the guy he tried to hammer. His bass glanced off the guy's shoulder and accidentally hit Ted Cohen flush in the face. The second time his bass swoops down, he hits photographer Richard Aaron in the forehead and Cohen again, this time on the bridge of his nose. Cohen falls to the floor. The only Warner Brothers employee willing to get anywhere near the Sex Pistols, he has paid dearly for his commitment.

Suddenly, the power in the club flickers and switches off. The stage crew leap for the band, ready to pull them out of the club, fearful of an imminent riot, but by the time the lights and sound return thirty or forty seconds later, the mood has changed. Vicious's outburst and the electrical-system glitch have gotten the crowd on the band's side. Full beer cans still make their way to the stage, but they are being thrown by people with smiles on their faces. This is the crowd's idea of fun. The band members negotiate around the piles of garbage.

After the lights return, the security crew notices some film

cameras. Within seconds, Forcade's film crew are being vio-
lently ejected from the club. (Like McLaren, Forcade won't actually come in to the club. He's waiting outside.)

Outside, Forcade and his team fight back, flailing at the
security guards. They've followed the band for five days now
and are still getting thrown out of shows. Forcade is fuming.

"You can't get away with this shit!" he yells as he's being
thrown onto the street. "Don't you fucking know who I am?"

Back in the club, Johnston stands on the side of the stage
behind the public-address-system stacks, in order to avoid getting hit by the cans and bottles. Next to him stands a local
sheriff. Bottles continue to fly. One hits the sheriff in the head
and knocks off his cowboy hat. As he staggers from the impact, he reaches for the gun by instinct. He quickly recovers.

Johnston is worried about being so close to someone so
anxious to use a gun, so he leaves and walks through the
crowd to the sound board. He finds that no one is controlling
the sound. It must have gotten so violent that Boogie has left
the board. The sound is horrible, and there's complete may-
hem onstage. Sid is completely covered in blood, beer, and
mustard. By the end of the show, the stage is knee-deep in
bottles, cans, and other garbage.

2 A.M.

A major food fight ensues backstage. The band members
come into the backstage area after meeting outside with a few
sedate fans, and soon beer and sandwiches are flying every-
where. The band members get loaded and let off some steam,
having a wonderful time, just like their audience did a short
time earlier.

Although it was a tremendous, cathartic show and everyone is letting off their remaining steam, all are starting to get
fatigued. As the food fight winds down, Rotten pulls a vodka
bottle away from Sid and demands, "Sidney, why don't you
just straighten up? You're still wanking off with the fuckin'
drugs."

Sid doesn't respond and Johnny pushes the bottle back

into his friend's chest. Friend? Everyone—the crew, the band, the press, Forcade—is getting nastier. Everyone has chosen sides.

It's not just drugs that the Sex Pistols are arguing about tonight. It's been months since the band members tried to put together a new song. They've been playing the same songs in the same order every show for more than three months, and it's starting to turn into a routine, a ritual. This terrifies Rotten the most. No creativity, relentlessly grinding out the same tunes every night, turning the numbers emptier and emptier. This is what he set out to condemn and destroy. To Rotten, Jones and Cook are mere sidemen, with no ideas worth touching, and Vicious has earned the nickname "fucking useless." And McLaren is no help. McLaren won't help push the band to move forward—he's having too much fun flying from town to town and imagining headlines. This isn't a band, Rotten thinks, this is a bloody circus. And I'm not going to be anybody's bloody clown.

Rotten moves outside and holds a brief, impromptu press conference.

"The audience was a bunch of fuckin' statues tonight."

One reporter says, "You should bring some people from England to show them how to dance."

"What?" Johnny asks, mentally sharpening his fangs. "That's a fuckin' stupid thing to say. That's a fuckin' stupid idea. Bollocks."

Another asks, "There were rumors that you were going to play Madison Square Garden for one dollar per person."

"Bullshit. Total bullshit. We were thinking about it, but we decided not to because it's such a shit hole. We'll never play big shit holes like that."

"But what if a lot of people want to see you?"

Rotten takes the opening. "Yeah, *see* us. That's all they could do. That's not what it's about."

"Is it true that you believe that the CIA is following you?"

"Yes. Of course they are."

"What makes you think so?"

"It's not hard to spot them. They're just fat pigs who try to look cool and fit in. Now if you will all excuse me, I want to be left alone." He limps back to the food fight.

3 A.M.

Back at the hotel, the band members let out some of their frustration—once again, on Ted Cohen, who is resting in his room, recovering from the night's earlier wounds.

The band members are back at the hotel to pick up their belongings for the overnight drive to Baton Rouge. (Just to play it safe, they're not spending even one night in San Antonio.) They knock on Cohen's door just before they leave.

"We just want to say good night to you, mate," one says. Cohen, who is staying over at the hotel and flying to Baton Rouge tomorrow, reluctantly opens the door. Vicious, Rotten, D.W., and Monk run in and toss anything they can find across the room.

Sid, Johnny, and D.W. jump on the bed. Ted screams and screams. Noel cries, "Sid, catch!" and throws the night-table lamp at him. Sid executes a perfect drop-kick. The lamp splatters off the ceiling. Everyone runs to the corners to escape the flying glass.

Teddy shouts, "You motherfuckers! I'm gonna get you!"

"Great, huh?" Sid asks Johnny as they leave the room.

"Shut up, Sidney," comes the response. "You're fucking useless. You can't play. You're so fucking stoned all the time. You can't keep it together."

"Bollocks," Sid sneers. "Fuck off."

CHAPTER NINE

Day Seven: Monday, January 9—Baton Rouge

7 A.M.

DURING THE ALL-NIGHT DRIVE from San Antonio to Baton Rouge, Sid has once again disappeared.

"Did you stop at all?" a groggy Monk demands of Charles after he scours the bus, looking into all the bunks, for Vicious and comes up empty-handed.

"Just for gas," Charles says. "I never opened the door. I'm not that dumb. Sid couldn't have gotten out."

Monk and D.W. stalk the center aisle of the bus and check to see if any emergency windows have been opened wide enough for Sid to disembark. No luck.

There's no place he could go if he jumped out while Charles drove west across Louisiana. They've traveled through bayou country; the land here is so soft and spare that most of the highway is bridge. If Vicious jumped off, he'd be swimming.

"I'm gonna take a leak," Monk tells D.W. "I'll be right back."

"You better zip in and zip out," D.W. calls back. "The chemicals stink."

Yet the chemicals aren't the only smell that smack Monk as he opens the bathroom door and sees Sid on the toilet, stuck to the seat, leaning against the wall. He's doubled over, hours-old vomit solidifying on his mouth.

"Hi, Noel." Sid slowly looks up then pulls his head back down. "I need some smack. I need some bad. And I better wipe m'self."

Noon

As Ted Cohen checks out of the San Antonio Broadview Plaza, he notices a few extra charges on his bill:

damaged bedspread	$45.15
destroyed lamp shade	13.50
labor on glass cleaning	10.00

Fun on the road, as he might say.

5 P.M.

Fatigue has begun to set in, hard. The band members stayed up all night on the bus, checking out whatever minor sights there are to see on the trip through southeast Texas and west Louisiana to Baton Rouge, smoking and drinking, and posing for Polaroids with the band's new mascot: an anatomically correct blow-up doll one of the security men picked up at a truckstop. The band's attitude is adamantly anti-sex, but this is their toy. Everyone is content to sleep on and off and lounge around their Baton Rouge hotel, keeping to his own vices.

The only positive note of the day, as far as the band and crew are concerned, is that Sid has taken his first bath since he arrived in America. He still spends much of his time deciding on the right combination of talcum powder and Vaseline for his hair, but at least his presence isn't immediately revolting anymore.

After his bath, Sid meets up with photographer Roberta

Bayley. (Forcade has found the Sex Pistols' hotel.) Bayley, who believes in all the do-it-yourself good that has come out of punk, talks to Vicious about all the alcohol she's seen him drinking.

"You really ought to cut it out a bit," she suggests warmly.

"Ah, it ain't nothing," Sid says. "It ain't nothing to me."

The conversation soon escalates into a friendly wrestling match.

"OK, I'll fight with you," Bayley says. She's thin; she'd be no match for Sid. "But don't make it rough. Don't kick."

"I won't kick."

"Do you promise?"

"I promise I won't kick."

Within a minute, Sid kicks Bayley in the hand, breaking her nail.

"You said you wouldn't kick."

Vicious stops himself cold and offers a dozen heartfelt apologies in thirty seconds. "Go ahead. Kick me. Come on. Kick me. I deserve it." He didn't hurt her badly, but the intensity of his apology suggests he thinks he kicked her hand off.

This is the state Sid is in. He wants to relate to people and he thinks the only way to do it is to fight them. He's capable of promising something one second and forgetting it the next. He means no harm, but he is out of control.

Meanwhile, McLaren is doing what he does best: disseminating creative disinformation. He's organized a little press conference in his suite—catered by Warner Brothers— and he's having a ball. The plans he conveys are absurd to say the least. According to McLaren, the Sex Pistols are recording a film and a live album based on their American tour, they're furious at Warner Brothers for lack of support, and they're preparing for an extensive tour of Puerto Rico.

7 P.M.

At the early evening sound check, Sid is still reeling from the morning's sick spell. He's drinking beer and running across the hall, knocking down chairs, and generally acting wild.

"Sidney," Rotten sarcastically intones from the stage. "It would mean a great deal to us humble musicians if you'd share your presence with us. We need your inspiration."

"I ain't doin' no fuckin' sound check. I don't need no fuckin' sound check. I'm Sid Vicious!"

"I don't care if you're fucking Eric Clapton," Rotten counters over the sound system. "Get your bloody bollocks on the fucking stage."

As Rotten talks, Red slips Sid's bass guitar over his head onto him. Sid doesn't mind, absent-mindedly hitting strings as he walks in wide circles.

Sid looks down at his bass and says, "I can't do a sound check with this horrible guitar strap on my bass. This strap, it's horrible. I'm Sid Vicious. I want a guitar strap with my name on it."

"Sid," Monk intrudes. "Do the goddamn sound check and I'll buy you a guitar strap with your name on it."

"All right then." Sid takes the stage and the band leans into a ragged, elemental version of "Belsen Was a Gas."

"I don't know why they bother doing sound checks," Red tells Monk. "It's gonna sound like shit tonight no matter what. You think Boogie's gonna make sense outta this?"

"No shit," Monk says. "Listen, you don't have to stay around if you don't want to. Why don't you go into town and pick up a leather guitar strap for Sid?"

8 P.M.

Jim Rink and a friend open a bag of tomatoes they bought on Friday. The tomatoes have gone bad and smell horrible. But Rink and his friend aren't hungry; they bought these tomatoes to throw at the Sex Pistols.

Rink, age thirty, owns a record store called the Record Rink that's just around the corner from the grocery-store-turned-club, the Kingfish (nicknamed after Huey Long), that the Sex Pistols are playing tonight. Rink is also a musician, and he is heavily influenced by techno-rock practitioners like Yes and Emerson, Lake, and Palmer. He admires the people who he considers wizards. He gives such records premium space at his shop. He's an art-rock evangelist for all who will listen.

Rink isn't going to the Kingfish tonight because he likes the Sex Pistols. He has a plan. He's going to smuggle his tomatoes into the club, stand at the back of the club, and throw them at the stage when he gets his chance. It'll be his personal statement. How dare these brats who can't play a note invade his territory? Rink isn't a violent man; the tomatoes will be his protest.

10 P.M.

The fatigue that has enveloped the Sex Pistols also has a deleterious effect on tonight's show at the Kingfish. It's the first one at which the band seems indifferent, which makes the unsettling thoughts in their music that much more unsettling. What could be stranger and less authentic than a band screaming for anarchy and destruction when the band members are clearly bored? Rotten likes to skewer the rich Rolling Stones for having the arrogance to still sing "What can a poor boy do/Except sing for a rock and roll band" (from the ten-year-old "Street Fighting Man"), but what the Sex Pistols are doing right now isn't all that different.

Johnny Rotten's fears about the band's deterioration come alive on stage. There's hardly any interplay among the Sex Pistols; everyone stands in his set place, plays what he's supposed to, and keeps to himself.

Yet the crowd at the Kingfish seems unaware of any inertia on the band's part. Baton Rouge has never seen anything like this before. The Sex Pistols on a bad night are still a revelation for the uninitiated. The ideas that scream from these songs—I wanna be anarchy, You're vacant, We mean it man—are unprecedented in their directness and determination.

That's why Jim Rink experiences a revelation as he cradles his tomatoes. As the sound rushes by him, he realizes that the music he hawks at the Record Rink doesn't touch people because it isn't fun. This is fun, playing loud and fast and dirty. And if you listen to the words, you can hear that the Sex Pistols can make a statement and be fun. Rink throws his tomato at the stage (it smashes inside Cook's bass drum), but he does so to become part of the show, not to attack it. Tonight this thirty-year-old premature curmudgeon sees and hears that the music of those a decade younger is still viable. Rink, a man who has memorized more blues scales than he'd like to admit, doesn't care that Steve Jones isn't the best guitar player he's ever seen. The following morning, Rink plans to throw away his Emerson, Lake, and Palmer records and redesign his store. His whole record collection will change. He'll start listening to music that's fun. He'll start having fun.

It's less fun under the stage lights, all red and amber, except for the stark white image that Rotten offers. The garbage on stage tonight is heavy on the seafood, and the stage reeks.

Jones, Cook, and Rotten are so wrapped up in themselves and escaping the moment that they don't notice what happens midway through the set on stage right. Sid, the only member of the band who's interacted with the crowd (granted, the interaction consists of insults and graphic requests for female companionship), leans into the audience and pulls onstage one of the few genuine punks in the audience. (The audience, much of it imported from New Orleans, comprises mostly young, professional white men hoping to catch a freak show.) She's short and unattractively hefty, and she's thrilled to be pressed up against the stage. She's content to be in front of Sid, dancing, working closer. Either the security crew is content to leave her alone or they don't want to have to touch her.

Between songs, she shares vodka with Sid and french-kisses him, each time more passionately. During "New York," she leans closer with half her body onstage and closer to Sid, finally falling to her knees in front of him. Sid twists his bass behind him, giving her easy access to his crotch. She has Sid's jeans halfway to the floor boards before the promoter calls on Monk to pull her off to the side of the stage. The usually vigilant Monk, standing only ten feet away from Vicious, hasn't noticed what Sid is up to. Like the rest of the audience, he's transfixed by Rotten's performance and doesn't notice anything else.

Monk helps Sid pull his pants back up. Sid is oblivious; he stands limp (well, mostly limp), barely aware of what is happening around him. He doesn't push back. Through all this, "New York" continues; no one else in the band cares if there's no bass. Just play and get it over with.

The tension isn't between band and audience tonight—it's within the band. They don't even look at each other. But there's tension in the crowd. Once again, Forcade's lackeys are thrown out of the show. Once again, Forcade stands outside, threatening violent retaliation. "I'm not fucking kidding anymore!" he shouts. "I'm getting even! This film is going to happen!" But he's left outside. The security guard has ripped his expensive western-cut jacket. Now he's really mad.

Like Memphis, Louisiana has its own musical history, one that made the Sex Pistols possible. Second-line New Orleans rhythm-and-blues rhythms and Cajun zydeco shouts from the bayou both were musical movements by the people and for the people. Performers as varied as New Orleans' Huey "Piano" Smith and zydeco accordionist Clifton Chenier made music that for years was ignored by the major record companies, music that tried to capture everyday hopes and desires. The links from them to the Sex Pistols, today's chroniclers of everyday hopes and desires, are easy to discern. But don't tell that to the old-timers. They don't want to have to pay any attention to the everyday events that the Sex Pistols choose to sing about, from sexual degradation ("Sub-mission") to abortion ("Bodies") to war ("Holidays in the Sun," "Belsen Was a Gas"). The Sex Pistols sing forbidden thoughts. These are everyday thoughts for ugly times.

Someone throws a half-dozen coins at Rotten's face. "Fuck this!" he cries. "No coins! Where's the hundred-dollar bills?"

The band members are once again in a city that should on some level be attracted to them, but Baton Rouge wants the Sex Pistols no more than Memphis. The Sex Pistols are too extreme. Although there are some in Louisiana who can make the connection and might be open to the band, what they see on stage is too repulsive to follow. The Sex Pistols are the extreme end of the music they love, and the audience is appalled, both by the music and what it means about the listener's musical beliefs. The Sex Pistols don't help themselves by delivering a distant, jaded performance.

Midnight

Backstage at the Kingfish, the band members try to avoid thinking about how disappointing the show was. Jones picks his pimples; Rotten scours the backstage area for people he can bait. McLaren picks up a young groupie. Johnston and Monk fight over a videocassette recording of the show that Glen Allison confiscated; Johnston wins, but not until the argument escalates into a screaming match. Sid drinks a bit, then walks onto the club floor.

Vicious and Rotten are old friends, but it has become apparent that the reason they work together so well as Sex Pistols is their incompleteness when they're apart. They are two halves of the same person, Sid being the physical side and Johnny the cerebral. Rotten is all taunts, but he shies away whenever violence looms; Vicious can interact with people only through physical contact. They may hate each other nowadays—Rotten's admonitions that Vicious stay away from drugs becoming more hurtful and less constructive by the day—but they need each other. As Ian Hunter sings (or Forcade's mentor Norman Spinrad writes), you need two wings to fly.

The club is far from empty. Many reporters have been waiting for nearly an hour for the press conference with the band that McLaren has promised them. When Sid inadvertently walks past them, they clamor for his attention. The security force gets overzealous, but doesn't eject the reporters. Several dozen fans are still in their seats, dazed from the performance.

In the main room of the club, Vicious reunites with the short young woman with dark hair as spiky as his whom he had pulled onstage earlier. The lust-filled couple can't climb onto the stage because the crew is taking apart the band's equipment, so lanky Vicious drags this five-feet-three-inch, 160-pound package of bulging spandex, the new fabric of choice for groupies, onto the club's bar and throws himself atop her. They switch positions and she begins to take him in her mouth. Sid smiles, lays back, and takes an occasional swig of his beer.

The promoter's assistant sees this happening and is horrified. He runs backstage and tells Monk to get his security people into the hall. They have to shove through a crowd to get back to Sid. All the fans are watching, and the reporters and photographers are in full force. Some are taking photographs. It's a real confrontation; the press is sick of the lack of access Monk has afforded them and Monk is furious that so much press is badgering the band. Angry words are exchanged, lines are drawn, but it doesn't escalate to blows—for now.

Monk, Glen, and D.W. pull the woman off Sid and bring them backstage, through the photographers, past the main band area, farther down the long hall, into a ten-foot-by-eight-foot broom closet with a sink. The smells of sweat and sex swirling around the pair, they go at it there.

Rotten can't find anyone new to bait tonight, so he contents himself with the security crew. He's angry at the audience ("They didn't make us want to do anything up there"), angry about tour logistics ("We were already in Texas once. Why are we going back?"), angry at McLaren ("I've got my own fuckin' brain. I don't need McLaren's.").

While Rotten catches a kip, Cook talks to crew members about what McLaren has in store for the band after the American tour. Malcolm has started talking to reporters, quietly and with demands of nondisclosure, about bringing the Sex Pistols to South America.

Specifically Rio. Malcolm has been scheming the past few days, whispering to anyone who'll listen that he's figured out another great gimmick. He's going to fly the band down to Brazil, where they'll hook up with Ronald Biggs, one of the Great Train Robbers, who's in Rio having successfully fought extradition. Biggs is an old fixation for McLaren; back in his art school days he designed a Biggs T-shirt that he still sells back at the Sex shop.

It seems that Biggs fancies himself something of a poet, and the band will back him up as he reads his verses. Biggs is a genuine outlaw, the band members want to be perceived as outlaws. It's a perfect mix. Great idea, everyone nods, but what about Johnny, the Sex Pistols' lead singer? What's he going to do during all this? McLaren smiles and changes the subject.

CHAPTER TEN

Day Eight: Tuesday, January 10—Dallas

Noon

DURING THE ALL-NIGHT DRIVE from Baton Rouge to Dallas, the Sex Pistols' bus crosses the Mississippi River for the third time. Once again, it's too dark to discern scenery. They might as well paint it on the windows to give themselves something to look at.

The Sex Pistols have seen enough biker movies and westerns. As they ride northwest to Dallas, they're ready to see a genuine Texas truckstop. To them, that's real Texas. They're also hungry.

Everyone is uneasy as they enter the vast truckstop. Bus driver Charles and photographer Gruen won't even sit near the band. If there's going to be any trouble, they just want to drink their coffee quietly at the counter.

The waitress takes her time getting to the band, and pays for her tardiness.

"Cunt, I'm hungry!" Sid shouts. "I want my food and I want it now!"

The waitress's jaw drops to the floor, as do many others. Sid is wearing a dirty white T-shirt with promotional buttons and skin-tight leather jeans. The clientele braces.

The truckstop is filled with fifty truckers, all of them staring at the band. The other band members freeze, certain their lives are about to end. Monk knows he'd better straighten out

Vicious before someone else gets the idea. He backhands Sid in the stomach hard to get his attention.

"This woman works real hard for a living!" Monk shouts two inches from Vicious's ear. "You can't talk to her like that! She's a real nice lady! She'll give you whatever you want, but be polite!" He says this as loud as he can, so everyone there can hear that the perpetrator is being disciplined.

"I'm sorry," Sid says to the waitress. "I'm really sorry. It's just that I'm hungry. I'm really sorry."

"Whadd'ya want?"

"I want steak and eggs."

"How ya want 'em?"

"I want me steak rare and me eggs runny."

A full twenty minutes pass without incident.

After Vicious devours his meal, a small mountain of steak and eggs, he grabs Monk's hamburger. Sid takes a big bite and turns green. "Mate, where's the loo?" Monk points, and Sid runs. Sid gets to the men's room just in time and vomits all over the wall.

The crew realizes this is the way it is going to be for the rest of the tour. Vicious is going through a bad withdrawal and he isn't going to keep much food down.

It's before noon and Vicious has already been through a six-pack of beer, which is also all over the wall.

They walk back to the table and sit. Sid has a milkshake to settle his stomach. Then back to the bus.

Back in Baton Rouge, Cohen boards a Delta flight to Dallas along with McLaren. They're tired, so they don't talk much. They certainly aren't causing any trouble. Before they even reach their seats, one of the flight attendants begins lecturing them. By now, nobody bothers to wait for anyone associated with the Sex Pistols to cause trouble. The word is out.

6 P.M.

At the Greenleaf Hotel in Dallas (the band is supposed to be staying at the Ramada Inn Convention Center), Vicious is being bathed by the security crew. They have become so paranoid about Sid's well-being that they won't even let the boy take a bath by himself. Several members of the crew stand outside the bathroom and watch.

A member of the road crew returns from a trip downtown. He's frazzled.

He tells everyone that he spent the afternoon at a massage parlor. "Get this: I hung my pants over the door and got a fucking great massage." He describes this in significantly greater detail. "When I got up and put my pants on, I found out that I lost my wallet. All my fucking money is gone. Should we call police? How will I get my stuff back?

The story has a punch line. "But it wasn't all bad. Those nice women, they let me have my massage for free."

In the lobby, Monk shares a friendly chat with Monty, a British photographer following the tour. Monty is considerably older than the rest of the entourage, and he's the only one who doesn't treat the Sex Pistols in a confrontational fashion. To the road crew, Monty is the only person from the British press who has any class. Monk has helped Monty in the past. At the San Antonio show, he pulled Monty back from the rafters at a time when it seemed the crowd was about to storm the area.

This afternoon, Monty returns the favor.

"I hear you've been having some trouble with Forcade," Monty says.

"Yeah."

"Well I heard two of the guys in his film crew talking about some goons Forcade flew in. They said Forcade was having them come in to 'take care of the Warner Brothers people.'"

"So?"

"I think they meant you."

"Oh."

If Forcade's shenanigans in Memphis are any indication, this might be true. Monk thinks for a moment, and begins to plan his defense.

9 P.M.

Behind the parking lot of the Longhorn Ballroom is an area called Boot Hill. According to the signs around it, many prominent Texans are buried there.

The parking lot is a madhouse. It's freezing outside and snow is starting to fall, but a naked woman poses atop a Corvette for television cameras. As the promoter's son walks into the club, a live television camera captures a Sex Pistols fan spitting on him.

The legal capacity of the Longhorn is two thousand. Tonight, just over seventeen hundred people have bought tickets. Wary of a confrontation, the club manager supplies bartenders with only paper cups. No cans or bottles. There have also been rumors that the Sex Pistols set objects on fire during their show. The police and fire departments are here in full force to prevent it. The city health department is here too, with orders to prevent people from spitting.

"No one really knows what to expect," says police director E. Winslow Chapman. "We have been advised that they have been known to perform simulated sex acts on the stage. This will not be tolerated. It's purely precautionary. We don't want any trouble and we don't want to cause the Sex Pistols any trouble. If someone wants to pay their money to be spat on or vomited upon, then that's their business."

11 P.M.

The Sex Pistols are starting to tire of Americans, starting to hate each other, starting to hate their manager, starting to hate their predicament. They know, or at least Johnny Rotten knows, how poor and pro forma their Kingfish show was. Tonight at the Longhorn Ballroom, they're doing what they've learned to: They're working out their anger and frustration through the music, like rock-and-roll bands are supposed to.

To the three-hundred hard-core punks in front, this is the apocalypse they've been waiting for. (As usual, most of the audience is made up of curiosity-seekers. As the Dallas

Morning News states the following morning, "Most of the people last night came to see the people who came to see the Sex Pistols.") Rotten, shaking a black-gloved left fist, means no good and the punks are loving it. Taking Doreen Cochran's Atlanta words to heart, Rotten changes the words of "Anarchy in the U.K." to "Anarchy in the U.S.A." His evil stare screams I Have Come For Your Children!

"Look at that," Rotten says to Vicious, gesturing to the crowd, transferring all his anger to them. "A living circus."

Sid walks to the center microphone. "Dance you fuckers, you faggot cowboys."

Out of habit, the band returns for an encore. "You must be fuckin' mad to want more of us," Rotten suggests, and then calls for a pummeling version of the Iggy and the Stooges' self-explanatory protopunk anthem "No Fun." Backstage, Rotten has changed into a black T-shirt with a red swastika blazing through it. Someone gave it to him; he doesn't understand what it truly represents. After the song collapses, Rotten and Vicious pick up what items of value have been thrown onstage, and the Sex Pistols head back to a dressing room to decompress.

"This is great," Rotten deadpans. "I make more money picking up money than I do from performing."

Backstage, Rotten huddles with Bob Regehr, who has flown in from Los Angeles for the Dallas show. Rotten is clearly Regehr's favorite in the band. He has the star charisma Regehr always ferrets out.

By now, Forcade's crew have been through the nightly ritual of being thrown out the back door, sneaking back in, and being thrown out again. Ted Cohen is so aggressive pushing them out that he accidentally breaks one of the camera lenses. But at least Forcade's cameraman has a lens that can be repaired; while she was looking away, Annie Leibovitz's bag of cameras has been stolen.

What really galls Forcade is that a real camera crew commissioned by Warner Brothers has shot the show for future use. Three cameras—one fairly close to the front, two in back—have the whole thing in living 16-millimeter color. Forcade is furious: There's a full show in the can and it's not his.

Monk hasn't paid much attention to the show. He's worried that Forcade's goons are going to derail the tour—for good.

Monk and D.W. are waiting for violence backstage at the Longhorn, in the most violent city in America. America and the world know Dallas from the TV show, *Dallas.* The show offers up a city of violent, craven oil barons and enough decadence to make Sodom and Gomorrah look like nursery schools.

But if there's TV violence everyone knows about, there's also the real thing. The country considers Dallas a city of hate. Back in November 1960, Lyndon Johnson and his wife Lady Bird were jeered and jostled by an angry, partisan mob. This is not the home of southern gentility. Ralph Yarborough, who served in the U.S. Senate from 1957 to 1971, writes, "The climate was just unbelievable. It was very violent toward leaders in the National Democratic Party. Though I was treated courteously there myself, the people were just as passionate as any time in the McCarthy years. It was just unbelievable that a civilized people could have been whipped into that frenzy."

The single, terrible act of violence that has made Dallas infamous is the assassination of President John F. Kennedy. (As Don DeLillo writes in *Libra,* the assassination was "the seven seconds that broke the back of the century.") For years, the rest of the country has held a grudge against the city. When Melvin Belli defended Jack Ruby for the murder of Lee Harvey Oswald, he frequently likened the city of Dallas to Nazi Germany.

This is all most Brits know about Dallas: the assassination and the TV show. This is why McLaren wants them here. There could be violence, which would be fantastic for the image. McLaren imagines the headlines back home: CITY THAT KILLED JFK ATTACKS THE SEX PISTOLS. Perfect.

That's fine for Malcolm, but the headline Monk is trying to avoid right now is the one that banners his own obituary. Monk and D.W. have a plan they think will work, but someone has to walk into the trap for it to succeed.

They hear a loud bang on the back door. Company. "There's our trouble."

The side door slams open against the wall and in walk two short, built Oriental men, followed by one of the cameramen and, then, Forcade himself, looking both smug and agitated. To Monk and D.W., the Oriental men look like martial-arts monsters.

If they're scared, they're not showing it. "Get the fuck outta here," Monk barks.

Forcade responds, "Fuck you, Noel. You had your chance to play along. End of this line, pal." He brushes snow off his brand-new jacket.

Monk sees that Forcade's cameraman is filming all of this. Monk steps forward and smacks the film camera out of his hands. It crashes to the ground.

"You don't know when to quit, do you?" Forcade says, oozing contempt. "You just don't know when to quit."

Forcade looks to the Oriental men and flips his hand. "All right, boys. Take 'em."

The pair step toward Monk and D.W. As they're about to try to attack, from the darkness far behind Monk and D.W. emerge the dozen Dallas city cops Monk had tipped off. They all have their hands on their guns.

Their sergeant looks at Forcade and his crew. He thunders, "Boys, one more step and we'll blow your fuckin' heads off."

The assailants stop. Forcade's jaw drops.

"Now, boys. Now. Turn around and get the fuck outta here. I give you three seconds. Move, move."

Forcade gets in a last taunt before he leaves. "This isn't it, Noel. You can't have the cavalry around all the time."

"Thanks for the warning, Tom."

1 A.M.

Forcade and his goons are gone, but the night is far from over.

Monk and D.W. are still wary, so they venture outside the back of the club to see if trouble is still around. It's cold and it's snowing—unusual for Dallas in early January but not unknown. They slog through an inch of snow.

Forcade's crew has departed, but Monk and D.W. spy a sight just as unwelcome.

Vicious has apparently reunited with Lamar, the woman who bloodied his face during the show, and he's getting into Lamar's beat-up Volkswagen and driving off with her and her two groupie friends. Under normal circumstances, this isn't much of a problem. It's a typical groupie story. Band member on the road meets willing women, drives away for a long night of sex and drugs, and returns in the morning with a story to share. Maybe he needs to get a shot. It happens all the time, it's normal.

But these aren't normal circumstances. The last time Sid ran away from a club it took twelve hours to find him and two more hours to deposit him in the city he was supposed to be in. Monk cannot let Sid out of his sight. The risk is too great.

Monk and D.W. run as fast as they can in the snow. The car can't go fast either. The tires on the Volkswagen are nearly bald, and it's skidding on the snow, making circles.

"Get out of here!" Sid screams. "I gotta get out!"

Before Lamar can gain control of the car, she feels Monk hanging onto the door and leaning through the open window. He reaches through the window, fumbles a bit, and pulls out the car keys. He tosses them to D.W., who throws them as far as he can into the snow. Then they drag Sid out the back door.

Sid thrashes a bit, then resigns himself to being held down by the pair. "Man, they wanted to party," Sid complains. "I want to fuck the bitch."

Monk loosens his grip on Vicious and replies, "All right, but don't go into other people's cars. What'd I say? Stay with me and you can do what you want. But I have to know where you are. You want to fuck the bitch. You can fuck the bitch."

"All right."

The girls lean out the windows of the Volkswagen and curse Monk and D.W. They curse back. Sid belches.

Monk and D.W. walk up to Lamar, who looks even meaner up close.

"Sid wants to fuck you," Monk tells Lamar, and gives her hotel directions. "Be there in an hour."

Lamar thinks over the proposition for a second. "OK," she answers. "And fuck you."

3 A.M.

Back at the hotel, Monk hears some banging sounds in the adjoining room and opens the shared door to Sid's room. Sid has somehow acquired a set of brass knuckles, and seems pleased with what they can do. He punches holes in the walls and furniture, and smiles a drunk's smile. Monk throws up his hands and walks downstairs to find Lamar.

Monk and Lamar return to find Sid punching deeper holes in the wall. Monk shouts, "Sid, you're gonna hurt your hand!"

Sid laughs. "Not with these dusters I won't, mate. They work great!"

Monk tries to avoid standing too close to Lamar and takes a deep breath. "They do work great, Sid. They're wonderful. But you've got to give them to me."

"No way. No fucking way. Toss it." He begins to think of Monk and Lamar as appropriate targets for the brass knuckles.

Another deep breath. "I'll trade you," says Monk. "I've got your blonde, but you've got to give me the brass knuckles."

"Really?" Sid is so concerned he has stopped punching the wall.

"Really. It's fair. The bitch for the brass knuckles."

Sid lets the brass knuckles drop. Lamar taps the door behind her and closes it halfway.

D.W. and Monk stay on the other side. Lamar is in with Sid almost all night. D.W. and Monk are overtired, bored, can't sleep. They want to sleep, but they are too wound up. They play cards.

They think about who they can mess with. It's been an exciting evening. Sid is happy, and they know exactly where he is. Nobody needs them. It's 4:15 A.M.

Monk and D.W. get to talking about how they feel about McLaren. Monk hasn't gotten over McLaren's refusal to see any of the shows or deal with Sid back in Memphis. Over cards, they decide the time is right to get even.

"Let's fuck with the manager," Monk says.

"Great idea."

In this predawn hour, it is clear that Monk and D.W. have become addicted to excitement. Their job is to control it, but they have become part of it. And, as the beer, fatigue, and dislocation kick in deeper and deeper, McLaren is a logical victim for them. As they see it, they've been putting in twenty-hour days while McLaren, who hasn't done anything remotely constructive, gets all the rest. He's a celebrity, or at least a media freak. It's payback time. They form a plan.

Monk and D.W. walk to Malcolm's door. They bang on it as hard as they can a dozen or so times. Monk yells, "Open up! FBI! Come out with your hands up!"

Inside, Monk and D.W. hear much scurrying around. The door creaks open. Out walks Malcolm, stark naked. He prances into the hall and says, "I didn't know you guys were FBI."

McLaren is drawn into the madness, too. He's so paranoid and disoriented he's willing to believe that the band's tour manager and bodyguard are FBI agents. Maybe he thinks Monk and Forcade are in collusion. The paranoia is contagious.

Monk and D.W. struggle to keep straight faces. Then, just as they have McLaren up against the wall, legs spread, out from McLaren's room meekly walks another one of the tour sycophants, dressed the same as Malcolm. At this point, Monk and D.W. can hold in their pleasure at Malcolm's humiliation no longer and are waking people on other floors with their laughter.

McLaren pushes himself off the wall, spins around, points his finger, and shouts, "You're not FBI!"

Still howling, Monk answers, "Yeah! We're going to go back and play cards. You can go back in and play your games."

CHAPTER ELEVEN

Day Nine: Wednesday, January 11—Tulsa

2 P.M.

McLAREN, JOHNSTON, AND THE British members of the crew fly American to Tulsa. Everyone else heading north suffers the day-long bus ride.

The band's bus isn't even going to stop at the hotel in Tulsa until after the show. The band is traveling directly to Cain's Ballroom. The American crew is fearful that someone working for Forcade will be waiting for them at every turn. They're not leaving the bus unless it's absolutely necessary.

By now, half the band and crew has come down with deep chest colds. Fatigue and phlegm rule. Rotten doesn't mind being sheltered by the crew and Vicious's condition certainly demands such treatment, but Jones and Cook deeply resent it. Both are street toughs capable of looking after themselves; neither of them is going to run off for good if one of the security guards looks away for a second.

"This is the last time we go anywhere on the fuckin' bus, Malcolm," Jones tells McLaren as he walks to the bus.

"Don't worry, my son," McLaren says. "After Tulsa, you will always be flying."

On the bus, Red is trying to convince Vicious of the virtues of hygiene. "Why don't you do yourself a big favor and take a fucking shower?"

"A shower would be a good idea," Monk chimes in, blow-ing smoke into Vicious's face. "Think of how much more snatch you could have if you didn't look like a mess. Maybe you could wash away some crabs. Put 'em up for sale."

"Fuck you, Monk," Vicious says in as good-natured a fashion as one can convey those words. "I'm doin' fine with the birds." He points toward the front of the bus. "Charles is gonna do great, too, even better'n me, after we get him an electric guitar, get him into the band."

He smiles to underline his point, then points to the "I'm a Mess" button on his T-shirt. "You know that my hair's just now starting to look good. You think I'm gonna ruin it with a shower? Bollocks to that."

By now, Vicious has developed a ritual he keeps to any time he is about to be in the public eye. Every time he is about to get off the tour bus, he dips his hands in a jar of Vaseline, solidifies the spikes in his hair, dusts some talcum powder on it, and asks all within earshot whether his hair passes the test. He's working his hair hard.

"Forget yer bleedin' hair." Rotten doesn't enter the conversation so much as he intrudes upon it. He's a few feet back, but he's taken in the whole talk.

"Get off it John," Vicious shoots back. "What do you wanna talk about?" Vicious then leans into an accurate impersonation of his disheveled friend. "How absolutely bawww-ring everything is? How absolutely bawww-ring America is? How absolutely teee-dious it is being the famous punk-rock star Johnny Rotten, the leader of the absolutely teee-dious Sex Pistols?"

Rotten stands up and begins walking toward Vicious.

For once, Jones and Cook aren't looking down at comic books, staring out the window, or tossing around the band's inflatable-groupie mascot. They're deep into this confrontation. They've been talking about this moment, waiting for it virtually since Vicious joined the band. Rotten wasn't in the group when they started. He didn't even work in Sex. Who made him the boss? Certainly not Malcolm.

They both know that the major songwriter in the band back when they were writing songs wasn't Rotten but Glen Matlock, Vicious's predecessor. Since Vicious joined the band, they've only worked up two new songs, "Belsen Was a Gas" and "Sod in Heaven," neither of which emit a fraction of the energy of even the lesser songs they hammered out with Matlock during seemingly long-ago rehearsal sessions. Musically, the band is falling apart—even if Sid has taken the time to learn to play as many as half the songs in their set.

The two principals of the band are finally going at each other. One's a junkie who can't play a lick; the other is the most unpleasant, pretentious person (other than McLaren, of course) they have ever met.

"Yer both jes cunts," Jones lets out.

"I didn't ask the backing band what they thought." Rotten gives Jones his patented stare. Jones spits toward it.

"I'm not a fuckin' journalist," Jones says after he's wiped his mouth with the back of his hand. "You can't make me disappear by starin' at me."

"I know you're not a fuckin' journalist," Rotten says. "Journalists may be cunts, but at least they do something. That's more than I can say for you lot. Why don't ya earn yer keep?"

"All right, King Johnny," Jones scowls. "Whatever you say, King Johnny. All hail Johnny Rotten, the useless King of the Punks."

Jones and Cook go into convulsions at this response. For once they've gotten at Rotten. It's a nice feeling.

"I'd talk to you," Rotten says to Jones, "but I fear you wouldn't be able to understand a single word that I say. So I'll spare you the embarrassment and move on to the next victim. Ta-ta."

Rotten walks down the aisle to Vicious. "And now for you, ya pathetic junkie. Nobody fuckin' cares what ya fuckin' look like because yer just going to smack it up and look like shit anyway."

Rotten walks closer. "Yer so utterly pathetic, Sidney, so absolutely pathetic. You should be in the fuckin' Rolling Stones, Sidney."

By now he is standing over Vicious, looking down at him. "Perhaps I'll phone Mick and see if there's an opening."

Sid doesn't respond; he curls his lip, spits on the floor, and looks away. It's not much of an escape, but it's something.

4 P.M.

Charles (who hasn't joined the band yet, if you were wondering) stops the bus for gas at a rest stop just north of the Oklahoma border. Rotten stays on the bus. His sinus problems have returned, and he looks even paler than usual. He leans back and explodes a pimple on the side of his mouth. Paul and Steve walk out of the bus and shoot their water guns at the gas station attendant. Bob Gruen rolls his eyes. He wants to go home.

"We'll sit at the counter," he tells Charles. "I don't want anyone to know that I'm with them."

Sid starts to walk down the steps of the bus and finds his way blocked by six hundred pounds of Glenn and D.W., both folding their arms, both staring at Sid, neither smiling.

"Don't worry, don't worry," Sid says, as he pulls his right hand through his hair in search of the perfect spike. "I promise. No problems."

"Better not be."

"It's no big deal. I'm just gonna get me m' steak 'n eggs."

As they walk into the small restaurant, they brush by a family, a couple in their mid-forties and their daughter, who looks eleven or twelve. The father, dressed in overalls and a flannel shirt, does a double take when he sees the entourage. He pulls his wife and daughter back into the restaurant and stands next to the group.

"Hey, I've seen you on the TV," the man says, pointing at Vicious. "You're famous."

"They're the Sex Pistols," he says when he leans down to talk to his daughter. "They're that famous band. I saw on the TV that they were in Dallas."

"I've never been to Dallas," the short, thin, freckled girl tells Sid.

"Where y'all goin'?" her father asks.

"Where we goin'?" Sid ask Noel.

"Tulsa," Noel replies.

"Tulsa," Sid tells the family.

"We've never been to Tulsa," the wife tells Sid.

"I wanna go to Tulsa," the girl says, and tugs on her father's arm.

"Maybe you can go to Tulsa with the Sex Pistols," her father says. "Say . . ." He turns to Vicious. "Why don't you take my daughter on the bus with you up to Tulsa. She's never been to Tulsa. She's never been with anyone famous."

By now, Sid has started slinking away toward a table, so the road crew has to give this man the unhappy news.

"I'm not sure that would be such a good idea," Monk says. "It might not be the best place for your little girl to be. We'd like to help out, but . . ."

"Sure," the man says. "I understand. Well, good luck in Tulsa."

"Damn," his daughter mutters.

Forty years later, two Okies have new heroes. The Sex Pistols are their new Bonnie and Clyde.

Sid, for once, gets through a meal without causing any damage to himself, the restaurant, or anyone around him. Of course he painted the wall of the bathroom with vomit, but that's old hat by now. By the time the entourage returns to the bus, it has begun to hail.

6 P.M.

Ted Cohen is waiting for a flight to San Francisco from Dallas-Fort Worth Airport. He's not going to Tulsa because he doesn't want to be dead.

This morning Monk received a call from Tom Forcade.

"Hello, is this Noel Monk?"

"Monk here. Who's this?"

"Your friend, Tom Forcade."

"What do you want?"

"I hear your associate Mr. Ted Cohen gave one of my associates some trouble at the show last night."

"Dunno what you're talking about."

"I hear he broke an expensive Bolex camera. Broke the damn thing in half."

"I don't know what you're talking about."

"Monk, the lens Cohen broke is going to set back my organization ten thousand dollars. If you don't pay me, I'm going to take care of him the same way I'm going to take care of you."

Click.

Ring.

"Ted?"

"Yeah?"

"It's Noel."

"What's up?"

"I think you might want to skip Tulsa."

8 P.M.

The Sex Pistols arrive at Cain's Ballroom. Charles stops the bus in front of the Holiday Inn just long enough for some crew members to enter the bus.

Waiting for the band are a few fans who drove down from Wichita, Kansas. (That hundred-and-fifty-mile drive is nothing for them; Bill Goffrier and his friends had to drive more than two hundred miles to Kansas City to scrounge up a copy of the Sex Pistols' "Anarchy in the U.K." single.) The area around the club is desolate, just the four guys from Wichita. An ice storm is in progress. The fans position themselves directly between the bus and the club; there's no way the band members can get through without acknowledging the fans.

Rotten is the first one out of the bus. His flu is raging and he's in an even worse mood than usual. He just barrels through. Cook and Jones come out next. They notice that the ground is icy and they start running down the street, sliding all over the place, having a ball.

Vicious is the last one out. He notices the fans and walks to them. He talks mostly to Bart, who in his black leather jacket looks the most like a punk.

"Nice Iggy button," Sid says, pointing to one of the many buttons on Bart's jacket.

"Thanks," Bart says. "You want it?" The fans all look up at Sid. With his hair spiked high and talced Sid looks taller to them than he really is. Couple that with their admiration for the band and he looks thirty feet tall.

"All right then," Sid says. "Pick one o' mine that you like."

Sid and Bart hammer out a trade. The fans are in awe. He seems gigantic; he has an overpowering presence. In their naïvete, they don't realize the physical condition Sid is in. Like many fans, they want to like the people behind the music so they can further justify their interest in the music. They always have to defend it anyway.

10 P.M.

The hail and sleet now add up to five inches. It's freezing in Tulsa tonight, but that hasn't deterred the Sex Pistols fans—or their detractors.

A group of religious protesters confronts the Sex Pistols outside Cain's Ballroom, another stop of the tour that is usually a country-and-western hall. The Bible Belt has a history of damning pop stars as Antichrists—ask anyone who burned a Beatles record over John Lennon's "We're bigger than Jesus" comment.

This is the first time the pickets have a literal confirmation of their theory. The first line of one of the songs, "Anarchy in the U.K.," is "I am an Antichrist!"

The thirty-odd young protesters, most of them from American Christian College or Oral Roberts University, carry large signs that read JESUS LOVES YOU and LIFE IS ROTTEN WHEN THE LORD IS FORGOTTEN and pass out leaflets that read:

"NO FUTURE FOR YOU!!!"
So says Johnny Rotten and it's not all lies—
Punk Rock exposes the joke of man trying to save
himself from the curse:
"THE SOUL THAT SINS WILL SURELY DIE."
So says God and he can't lie
NO FUTURE FOR YOU . . .
not in music, in social friends, in plans and good

deeds, and not in the rebellion that Punk Rock
peddles . . .
BUT
There is a Life and a Future Forever:
Jesus came to make a way back to
A FUTURE FOR YOU.
There is a Johnny Rotten inside each of us and
he doesn't need to be liberated—
he needs to be crucified.
Our sin nature must die at the cross of Jesus Christ
that we can be born again in the resurrected Christ.
TURN FROM YOUR PUNK WAYS
AND BE BAPTIZED INTO THE DEATH AND LIFE OF
JESUS . . .

Inside and around the hall, Forcade is of course nowhere
to be seen. After the Dallas debacle, he remains back at his
hotel, away from the action, free to maneuver.

Nonetheless, the previous night's face-off has apparently
intimidated Forcade's film crew. The crew is here, but they're
more interested in chronicling the protest outside than the
performance inside. After they get tossed out once, they've
had enough. Inside, the kids in the crowd were jostling them.
It's not worth the bother.

Not that they're missing much inside. The night's performance is a big step down from Dallas; the band is back on
listless automatic-pilot mode. Rotten's taunts to the crowd are
taunts of boredom, not outrage. He wants out. His bass player
is a junkie and the sidemen are replaceable. Cook lets the beat
waver and no one notices. As Baton Rouge proved two nights
ago, even a mediocre Sex Pistols performance is an experience
for the uninitiated.

As in Baton Rouge, the crowd doesn't care. For the opening act, a listless glitter-rock group, the hall security officials
keep the crowds off to the sides by the tables, keeping the
dance floor clear. They attempt to keep the floor free during
the headliner set, but when the Sex Pistols come out, everyone
rushes to the stage, bumping into cameras, bumping into each
other, slamming into the stage, loving every moment.

To Bill Goffrier and his friends, the music sounds surprisingly clear although they can see that Sid isn't playing much. Sid's most animated moment comes when he tries to repeat his San Antonio maneuver and slam his bass into the head of a heckler, but the stage crew stops him in time. Goffrier gets this all down on tape—he smuggled in a portable recorder—but he finds later to his chagrin that all he has is an unlistenable cassette. (Of course, one man's unintelligible cassette is another man's potential lucrative bootleg.)

The highlight of the show for Sid is after the encore, a stuttering "No Fun," after the other three members of the Sex Pistols have left the stage, when he picks out a tall blonde from the crowd.

"Come on, Sid," Monk implores, his arms wrapping Vicious's sweaty torso, trying to guide him to the backstage area.

"No, Monk," Sid says, holding his ground. "Remember we made a deal."

"What's the deal, Sid?"

"You said that if I don't jump into the crowd, you'll get me whoever I want."

"Is that what I said?"

Sid takes a swig of whisky and replaces the bottle in Noel's hand. "That's what you said."

"Then I guess I have to get you what you want."

Sid points out someone up front. "Monk, would you snag that one for me? I wanna do her. I wanna do that big bird."

"Are you sure?"

"I'm sure."

"She looks all right."

"She looks great."

Monk works his way into the crowd toward the woman Sid has pointed out. He hates walking through the nasty punks at the front of the floor—but this is his job. He arrives at the woman, and shakes his head at the intensity of the musk cologne she's wearing. She is taller than Noel and she has big, bulky arms, but she is attractive in the dark of the hall.

"I'm with the band," Monk shouts into her ear. "Do you wanna be with Sid?"

"Yeah," she shouts back in a low voice.

"Meet me in the lobby of the Holiday Inn in one hour."
He hands her a pass.

"I don't have a car."

"Then ride with us. Be at the back door in half an hour."

"No problem."

12:30 A.M.

In the bus on the way back to the hotel, Johnny curses at everyone for the night's listless performance. "Why don't you fuckin' try for a change?" he taunts. "You're all just wankin' off up there."

Nobody talks back; nobody cares.

Cook nudges Jones. "Looks like Sid got 'imself one big bird tonight."

"I dunno," Jones says. "He got 'imself somethin'."

2 A.M.

Vicious and the woman he chose at Cain's Ballroom have been in his room (as usual, he shares a suite with Monk) for forty-five minutes. The separating door bursts open, and Sid comes out, rearranging his black-leather jeans.

"I'm ready for the next party," he says, smiling.

"All right, wait one minute," Monk says. "Let me get her out of here."

As Monk walks in, Sid's companion is just starting to get dressed. On her right thigh, Monk sees a large scar, four inches wide by four inches long. The low voice and the big arms finally add up. Her leg was where she got the skin for her grafts done. She had once been a he.

"What are you checking out?" she grumbles.

"Oh, nothing," he said. "Uh, what do you do for a living?"

"I'm a stripper," she says as she finishes dressing herself and walks out. "I gotta go. I gotta strip at this club."

"How was it?" Monk asks Vicious as she closes the door behind her.

"I don't know. I wasn't sure if I was supposed to suck her cock or her cunt, know what I mean? Got m'self a big bird. Hey, can I have a vodka?"

Monk walks to his desk, pulls a vodka bottle off of it, and shows it to Vicious. He points his finger two inches from the bottom of the bottle.

"Do you see this imaginary line?"

"Yeah."

"Don't drink past this line."

"Fuck off," Sid laughs, and grabs the bottle. After taking a swig, he says, "I want to party. That guy from *Punk* magazine is having a party. I wanna go."

"Then let's go. And watch that line."

Defenses are down. Tonight is the only night of the tour that Monk and the crew aren't being completely hostile to Holmstrom and Bayley. They let the pair on the bus for a quick five-minute see-nothing look, and now they're on their way to a birthday party for Holmstrom. The whole entourage is at the party: the band, the crew, even some people from Forcade's film crew. For a short time, they're not at each other's throats.

Sid mingles. "What happened to your arm?" someone asks.

"Cut m'self shaving," Sid says.

At the party, *Creem* reporter Patrick Goldstein corners Vicious and Rotten. As usual when a microphone is before him, Vicious puts down the rock establishment, particularly the Rolling Stones.

"Keith Richards, big fuckin' deal," he says. "He's nothing but a pathetic junkie who goes to get his fuckin' blood changed. He oughta change his bloody face. I'd do it for him!"

Vicious is factually correct, but he's just created trouble for himself. "Oh, a pathetic junkie," Rotten mimics.

This is getting too close to home. "Don't say junkie," Vicious commands.

"I'll say what I fuckin' well please," Rotten shoots back.

Vicious kicks Rotten's chair out from under him. "Just don't go around screamin' junkie."

On the floor, Rotten shouts, "Junkie! Junkie! Junkie!"

With this, Vicious stalks out. "Monk, let's go."

They return to their room briefly, share a beer or two and a joint. Along with D.W. they move to the hotel lobby, where Sid spies a new girl. (This one is definitely genetically female.)

"Hey honey, whatcha doin'? I'm Sid Vicious of the Sex Pistols."

"I'm not that type of girl."

Seasoned road rats D.W. and Monk look at each other and smile. She notices. "Yeah, well fuck you, boys. I'm not."

"I didn't say nuthin'," Monk protests.

"Why don't you come up to my room with me?"

"I'm not that type of girl. I'll go in with you. I don't mind sitting and talking with you, but I'm not going to do anything with you."

Five minutes later, the two of them go into Sid's room. D.W. and Monk sit down in Noel's room. The door is open between the rooms.

D.W. and Monk start to play cards.

"Do you smell something?" D.W. asks.

"Naah," Monk responds.

They play a few more hands of blackjack. D.W. keeps winning and losing the same five-dollar bill.

"Do you smell smoke?" D.W. asks.

"Naah," Monk responds.

Another hand.

"It's getting real quiet in there," D.W. says.

"Maybe they're asleep," Monk says.

D.W. puts down his cards. "I'm pretty sure I smell something. I'm going to check in on Sid."

Sid's fine. Just as the woman said, they're just sitting there talking. What neither of them notice is that Sid has left a lit cigarette on the couch, and half the fabric on top is burning. It takes D.W. two buckets of water to put it out.

4 A.M.

Dawn isn't far away, but Monk and D.W. still can't sleep. They're still playing cards, still trading the crumpled fiver, while Vicious alternately talks and fucks the woman in the other room.

"Argh!" Sid calls from the other room. "Bloody well wash m'bed!"

D.W. says, "I'll get it. Let me check what's goin' on."

He walks into Sid's room and returns to Noel moments later.

"You're fuckin' not gonna believe this," D.W. says. He quickly backs out of Sid's room and shakes his head half a dozen times.

Monk chuckles. "After all we've been through, I'm not going to believe something?" He inhales. "Wait a minute. What's that smell? It's horrible. It's worse than anything on the bus."

"Noel, you're not gonna believe this." Monk stands up and walks into Sid's room.

"I don't believe it," he says.

Before him he sees the girl who claimed she wouldn't do anything covered from the top of her head to her chest in diarrhea. She had been giving head to Sid, who threw up and had a diarrhea attack in the middle of it. She runs past Noel and D.W. to the bathroom and slams the door behind her.

Monk and D.W., hardened men who've been part of almost every imaginable rock-tour ugliness, shake their heads. The smells are overpowering. They pry open Vicious's window and in swoops a punch of cold air.

As the first light sneaks through the edge of the window shade, Monk opens his window slightly to get some fresh air (it doesn't accomplish much) and finally collapses on his bed. He tells D.W. he's finally going to sleep.

"Good night, Noel," D.W. says, and throws a roll of toilet paper softly at Monk's head.

"Here, Noel," D.W. says. "Have seconds. Look's like Vicious's Crabs is gonna be able to open up a few more franchises just here in Tulsa. We're gettin' ourselves a nationwide chain here, don't you think?"

CHAPTER TWELVE

Day Ten: Thursday, January 12—Tulsa and Points West

10 A.M.

ROTTEN AND COOK SLUMP on their stools in the hotel coffee shop. Holmstrom, who's nursing a hangover, moves down the counter next to them.

Holmstrom shows them a copy of *Punk* magazine. Cook seems interested in it, but its presence awakens Rotten to his usual state of unmitigated cynicism.

"That magazine is disgusting. It's hideous."

"Shut up, John," Cook says.

"But it's disgusting. I've read it. It's absolutely hideous."

"Will you please shut up?

Vicious awakes in his hotel room in a foul mood. He's strung out, his stomach is giving out on him, his hair doesn't look right. His Holiday Inn room is overheated. It's ice cold outside, but the powers that be at the Tulsa Holiday Inn have seen to it that their guests wake up in an atmosphere that's either womblike or oppressive, depending on your attitude. Here it's more oppressive if you factor in the remains of last night's shenanigans. There's no temperature regulator in the room so the window is wide open. It doesn't help much.

Vicious asks for some food and Monk orders him his favorite—runny eggs and rare steak. But that doesn't calm Sid. When it arrives he complains about the food, complains about

Rotten, and tosses his breakfast tray across the room. The glassware splatters all over.

Monk acknowledges the disaster. "That was cute."

After Sid makes peace with what little can be salvaged of his breakfast, the entourage breaks into two. Steve and Paul fly with Malcolm to San Francisco, where the final show of the tour awaits them in two days. Johnny, Sid, and the usual bus entourage decide to take the non-stop cross-country trip by bus to Los Angeles, then drive up the famous California coast to San Francisco. They have two days to kill, and Sid and Johnny have made noises about wanting to see the country.

"In England, you can cross the whole country in a day," Vicious says. "There's more to see here. I want to see it. I want to see truckstops with cowboys and guns." Most of all, the bus presents a controlled environment that eases the crew's task.

As Rotten rides down the elevator to make his way toward the bus, he again meets up with Holmstrom, who is carrying a six-foot pair of longhorns.

"What the fuck is that?" Rotten asks.

"Longhorns, Johnny. They're for you. Do you want them?"

"Certainly, certainly."

"Then they're yours. A little gift from *Punk* magazine."

The elevator doors open.

"Hey," Rotten calls as Holmstrom begins to walk away. "Don't forget to slag us off in that magazine of yours."

"Don't worry," Holmstrom says. "That'll be easy."

1 P.M.

The bus passes a sign that reads DO NOT DRIVE INTO SMOKE and pulls into a Union 76 truckstop outside Oklahoma City.

The truckstop is enormous, with a sizable restaurant, gift shop, and shower area.

"Mr. Penniman," booms the loudspeaker at the front of the restaurant. "Your shower is ready."

There's no one to seat the group, so they set themselves at

a table under a sign that reads: PROFESSIONAL DRIVERS ONLY. PROFESSIONAL DRIVERS OPERATE ON A TIME SCHEDULE. THIS AREA IS RESERVED TO ASSURE THEY ARE NOT DELAYED. The crew tap cream containers back and forth. Rotten follows a minute later, slumps into his plaid suit, and discovers how deeply he can shove his finger into his left nostril.

After a round of hamburgers, Vicious and Rotten move to the adjacent gift shop. They've just received their per diems (twenty-five dollars a day, the most the band members have ever earned) and they plan to blow it all on badges and trinkets.

The Sex Pistols drop their fronts and enjoy themselves. They try on scarves and cowboy hats; they make faces and look at themselves in the mirror. They're kids having fun.

As they are about to leave the gift shop, each wearing some new totem, the middle-aged cowboy couple that runs the shop walk up to them.

"Ain't you the Sex Pistols?" the wife asks. "We think you're great."

"Hey thanks," Vicious says, and they're out the door.

"Pretty cool huh?" Vicious says to Rotten on the way to the bus. "Mum and Dad like us."

Rotten is less amused. "They *liked* us, Sidney." He mouths the words and tries to believe what he says.

"I know they liked us. Pretty cool, huh."

"But why would they like us?" Rotten asks. "We're not supposed to be liked."

"I don't know what you're talking about sometimes, John. You're up the tree."

The compliment is Rotten's worst nightmare. They have come to destroy a country's complacency, and two complacents have just given them their support. Johnny's head spins. Do I want them to love me or hate me? Am I Rod Stewart? Why are we doing this? What's the end result? His self-doubts continue to multiply, and there's no one on the bus with whom he can share them.

3 P.M.

For a change, McLaren has kept a promise he's made to Cook and Jones. Along with Johnston and Boogie, they're flying from Tulsa to San Francisco.

Because they made their reservations late, the four of them can't get seats together. Johnston takes one seat toward the front of the plane and the others sit a half-dozen rows behind him. Johnston is pleased; for two hours he'll have a short respite.

McLaren isn't using this time to relax. "Boys," he says to Jones and Cook half an hour into the flight. "How would you like to go on a little vacation?"

The kids are anxious. "Where to?

"South America."

"What's in South America?

"Train robbers, boys. Great train robbers."

McLaren doesn't get a chance to elaborate just yet; the stewardess is offering them lunch. The three of them all order chicken.

Five minutes later, as Johnston starts to eat his lunch, a chicken bone flies over his head.

Johnston is trapped in the middle of a row. He can't turn around to return the fire and he can't move. He resigns himself to Jones and Cook's antics and returns to his lunch.

Another chicken bone flies forward to the row and hits the person next to him.

"What the hell was that?" the passenger asks.

"Nothing," Johnston says. "Just a chicken bone."

Johnston looks up and meets the stare of one of the men in the flight crew.

"What are you doing?"

"I'm not doing anything, sir," Johnston says.

"We know who you are," says the flight officer. "You're a Sex Pistol."

The men on either side of Johnston move as far away as they can without leaving their seats.

"What?" Johnston argues. "I'm no Sex Pistol. I just work for them."

"That's even worse," the flight officer pronounces. "That

means you're responsible for them. I suggest you control your Sex Pistols or I will divert the flight to Santa Fe and have you all arrested."

McLaren, Jones, and Cook are laughing so hard that the flight officer turns to them.

"There had better not be another incident like this," he lectures. "And I'll tell you one thing. You'll never fly American Airlines again."

"Throw it at him," McLaren whispers to Jones, who's holding a chicken bone. "Let's see what happens."

5 P.M.

Half an hour ago, the bus passed through Clinton, Oklahoma. WELCOME TO CLINTON, read the sign at the city limits, WHERE JESUS CHRIST IS LORD.

"Bollocks!" Rotten shouts. "We're back in bloody Texas! What are we doing back in Texas?"

"I like Texas," Vicious says. "Tough cowboys. Look out the window."

Rotten looks out and sees a massive sign: RATTLESNAKES EXIT NOW.

"Let's get some rattlesnakes," Vicious says.

"Texas is pathetic," Rotten says. "Absolutely pathetic. Mr. Big Cigar, what are we doing back in Texas?"

Someone throws a map at Rotten, who discovers that the bus has to go through the top of Texas, through Amarillo, to get west into New Mexico.

"Whoever designed your lovely country was a fuckin' moron," Rotten observes. The crew is huddled in the front of the bus.

Rotten has to move forward to see them because the smoke from the many cigarettes everyone has been smoking is thickening. "I've only seen one thing from this place worth taking home: those longhorns that fool from *Punk* magazine gave me."

D.W. looks up from his card game with Monk and Allison. "Longhorns? Those can be pretty expensive."

"They're lovely," Rotten says. "My mother is going to love them."

"Longhorns," Allison says to his fellow players. "Big deal. Maybe he can wear them on his head."

The bus passes several packed killing fields right on Route 40 ("Look," points out Vicious. "Steak. Raw.") and just outside of Amarillo reaches the Cadillac Ranch.

Rotten looks out the window and is astonished. They are passing a dozen Cadillacs with the first two feet of their hoods buried in the ground.

"Why would anyone do something like that?"

"It's art, Johnny," Red says.

"Oh," Rotten says, and adds, with pretend pomposity, "It's a stirring work."

"It's no 'God Save the Queen,'" Red says.

"Got that right, mate," says Rotten. "Besides, I'd rather have longhorns on me head than a Cadillac with its face in the ground."

6 P.M.

"Bob Merlis, please. . . . Hello, Bob? This is Rory Johnston. We're in San Francisco."

"Where are you staying?"

"We're at the Miyako, just like we said."

"You're kidding."

"What do you mean?"

"The Miyako called Regehr and said you weren't allowed to stay there. How'd you get in?"

"I did what I normally do. I checked into the hotel and put all the rooms under my own name."

Steve and Paul aren't as wild-looking as Sid or Johnny. They can be brought into the hotel with minimal fuss.

"I'd better call ahead to Noel to let him know there might be some problem checking into the hotel," Johnston says.

"I don't think we can do that."

"Why not?"

"I just talked to Carl Scott. We don't have a clue where they are."

8 P.M.

Rotten is still looking out the window.

"What's a bleeding Tucumcari?"

"Calm down, Johnny," Monk says. "It's just the name of a town. It's an Indian name. We're in New Mexico now."

"I wish he'd calm down," D.W. says as he drops another card. "Maybe if we gave him the longhorns to suck on he'd relax."

"Ah, he's just a kid in a weird country," Monk says.

"No problem," D.W. says, imitating Rotten.

Monk takes another puff of his cigar. "Who did Johnny say he got those longhorns from?"

"I don't remember," D.W. says. "Hey Johnny. Where'd you get the longhorns?"

"The geezer from *Punk*," Rotten says. "Holmstrom."

Monk taps himself on the forehead. "Oh yeah, that's right. The reporter. Your deal."

D.W. deals. They play a hand, another hand. They drink, they tell jokes.

"Your deal, Monk."

Monk takes the cards. Just as he is about to deal the cards, he places the deck down on the book they're using as a makeshift card table and starts stroking his moustache with his left index finger.

"Whatcha thinkin' about?" D.W. asks.

"That guy Holmstrom's from *Punk*."

"Yeah. So?"

"Isn't Forcade the guy behind *Punk*?"

"Yeah. So?"

"Think about it."

"Oh shit."

"I'd better look at them. Charles, pull over!"

Charles pulls over at an emergency stop a few hundred yards down the road.

Monk opens the cargo bay under the seats and out pops a huge, five-foot-wide set of plastic horns that must have set Holmstrom back two hundred dollars.

"Good-lookin' pair of horns," Red says as he carries them back into the bus.

Charles maneuvers the bus back on the road. "Why are you lookin' at the longhorns?" Rotten asks. "What's the problem here?"

"Holmstrom is from *Punk* magazine," Monk says.

"So what?" Rotten shoots back. "The magazine is disgusting but the longhorns are marvelous."

"Don't you get it? *Punk* magazine is put out by Tom Forcade."

"The fool from *High Times*?"

"Exactly."

"So what's he going to do with the longhorns?" asks Rotten. "Put drugs in them?"

Stony silence.

"So there might be drugs in them," Rotten says. "Big deal. I'm not gonna fuckin' smoke a pair of longhorns."

"We're dealing with someone who sends little Korean monsters out to kill you if you don't do things his way," Monk snaps. "It would be just like that prick Forcade to dump some heavy drugs on us without our knowing it. You should know by now that you're a target for the cops. Remember Atlanta?"

Rotten's protests calm down. His cruel smile disappears.

"We're doing it for your own good," Monk says and half-believes. "Don't you know that if we get busted smuggling drugs, we'll all go to jail for the rest of our lives?" That's quite an overstatement, but Monk is so paranoid, fatigued, and stoned, that it sounds plausible.

Knives in hand, Monk and D.W. begin to desecrate Rotten's beloved longhorns. They start slowly, cutting off the tips. They find nothing. They think about it for a moment and then slice off a bit more. Nothing. Another short wait, another cut. Still nothing.

By now it's clear that the horns are genuine, but paranoia rules. Finally, they go at it with such force it's as if they're attacking Forcade himself, not one of his possessions. They slice the longhorns into bite-sized pieces.

Again, they find nothing. They pile the pieces in one end of the bus; Monk and D.W. return to their card game as if nothing has happened.

This is useless, Rotten thinks. My sinuses are getting worse, my manager is a conniving lunatic, my record company has abandoned me, my bandmates are junkies or brainless, and the people paid to protect me are destroying my possessions. I have to get out of here.

CHAPTER THIRTEEN
Day Eleven: Friday, January 13—Coming into Los Angeles

10 A.M.

THANKS TO A RELIEF DRIVER, the bus has been barreling all night, through areas with prefab adobes as well as genuine Indian country. All around them is arid, empty. As the bus passes Kingman, Arizona, and enters California, all is quiet. For once, all have slept, fairly soundly.

Life slowly returns to the bus passengers. The smell of stale cigarette and marijuana smoke mingles with that of the bus's stopped-up toilet. And since they slept on the bus rather than at a hotel, nobody has changed clothes or bathed. There are sweeter smells to greet groggy men.

Rotten is waking up. He blows his nose and adds to the dozens of used tissues and food wrappers on the bus floor. Except for D.W., Rotten has the worst cold of anyone on the bus.

One member of the road crew decides that the best way to wake Sid is with a cattle prod he bought in San Antonio, fearful that the crowd would turn ugly.

Vicious's response is more surprise than rage. His only flash of anger comes when he's not allowed to use the prod on someone else. He talks rationally, discusses issues intelligently, and is easy to read. Simply, he's kicking junk. He and Rotten seem to be communicating easily, with one glaring omission:

There is no talk about their future together. Call it a punk-rock détente.

The bus closes in on Needles, California, but nobody has been in contact with anyone from Warner Brothers since they left Tulsa. There is a freedom in the lack of accountability to the label, especially considering that Scott and Regehr are furiously trying to contact the group.

Monk's decision to stay out of touch with the label is more than a little vindictive. He feels he hasn't gotten the support he needs. After his Memphis request for methadone, nobody even bothered to call him to say no. Maybe he'll check in when he gets to Los Angeles (where they plan to stop to shower and then head north); maybe not.

8 P.M.

Softly: "Pss. Hey, Noel."

Charles leans to the right from his seat.

"Yeah," Monk responds. "What do you want?"

"Sid asleep?" Charles asks just above a whisper.

"Yeah, he's asleep," Monk says. "What's up?"

Charles pumps up the volume a bit. "Sid keeps talkin' about me join' the band."

"Oh yeah, that's right. I remember. So?"

Charles turns away from the road to make sure that Sid is asleep, then asks, "Do I really have to do it?"

8:30 P.M.

When the band finally reaches Los Angeles and checks into a Holiday Inn in Woodland Hills half an hour outside of downtown for a quick change and clean, the road crew is treated to one of the tour's most welcome events: Vicious is taking a bath.

"What do I do with this fuckin' soap?!" Sid shouts with

glee. Allison takes it upon himself to remind Sid how to bathe. Soon the tub is covered with slime and bugs.

When Sid emerges from the bathroom, soaking wet and wearing a goofy smile, he strikes several muscle-man poses that are memorialized in Polaroids.

Vicious finally clean, Monk phones his friend Mario, the maître d' at the prestigious Hollywood rock club the Whisky a Go Go. Monk doesn't care who's playing at the club tonight (whoever it is, the Sex Pistols probably hate them), but he wants to give Rotten and Vicious a taste of the American rock scene. Their tour schedule has kept them away from the usual nightclubbing spots; tonight they're going to party.

The newly washed band and crew all slip into their filthy clothes and head to the Whisky. Mario has secured the Sex Pistols and their entourage front-row center seats, which they take amidst much commotion, most of it caused by the group. They bump into people's seats, inadvertently knock over people's drinks, and make disparaging comments about the entertainment as they make their way to their VIP table.

After no more than a minute at the table, Rotten removes his finger from his left nostril for a moment and complains, "These fuckin' people. This sucks."

"Give 'em a chance," Allison says.

"I've been giving American rock and roll a chance for too long. This is horrible. It's detestable."

"Do you want to go?" Monk asks.

"Yeah," Rotten says. "Let's get out of here."

"I wanna be at a club," Vicious says.

"All right," says Monk. "We'll try another club."

"Now," orders Rotten. "This is bloody awful."

The entourage rises and leaves. They make a grand entrance, they make a grand exit.

What Johnny and Sid don't realize is that tonight they've finally become the bored rock stars they dreaded they'd become. They got special treatment in a prestigious Hollywood club, ordered a tray's worth of drinks, complained loudly, and left in a huff. Overgrown spoiled children, real rock stars. John, Paul, Steve, and Sid are the new Fab Four.

"I'm real sorry about this," Monk says to the Whisky's Mario in the outer lobby.

"Don't worry about it," Mario says as he presents Monk with a bill to sign. "Boys will be boys." (According to the bill paid to the Whisky by Warner Brothers on January 18, this brief "promo party" cost $90.70. The group never even got around to imbibing the drinks they ordered.)

"Well, now the boys want to go to the Roxy," Monk says. "Could you call ahead?" Mario, more professional than bemused, calls the Roxy and reserves a table for four: Johnny, Sid, Noel, and D.W. No one else even wants to bother with another club.

At the Roxy, the group is entertained by a band featuring two of Soupy Sales's kids. Sid says from the table, "I wanna go on stage, too. We're not playin' tonight. Let's play."

"Go for it," Monk concurs.

Sid leaps onstage and tries to grab the bass player's instrument. They fight over it. Sid gives up and starts cavorting around the stage, slam dancing against the band members and the equipment. At that point, a dull set becomes an interesting show. People start applauding; the band and Sid are having a ball.

Three numbers later, Sid jumps off. "Enough of this shit."

When Sid stumbles back to the table, Johnny gives him a piercing stare and demands, "Sidney, you always have to fuckin' show off, you poseur. Whyn't you just toss it?"

They all watch the rest of the show, board the bus, and head north toward San Francisco and the rest of the band.

3 A.M.

The other half of the band has kept itself quite busy tonight. Bonnie Simmons, the program director for San Francisco's KSAN, is the only programmer for a major-market commercial rock station that has embraced punk rock as anything but a fad to be laughed at and then ignored. The station's support of punk rock (and the intensity of the response) has much to do with area promoter Bill Graham's decision to book the Sex Pistols in his Winterland Theater. KSAN integrates punk into its usual eclectic mix; the station also offers *The Outcastes,* the country's first commercial-station punk-rock show, hosted by Norman Davis with Howie Klein, Saturday mornings from midnight to 2 A.M.

It's a charmed time for the staff and audience of KSAN. They all feel they're riding the crest of something that's about to break the rock industry in two. KSAN plays defiantly anti-commercial music that is attracting a significant audience, and the station halls are filled with excitement that they're on to something before any of their competitors, in San Francisco or elsewhere.

Tonight on *The Outcastes,* the station has made the mistake of inviting Sex Pistols Steve Jones and Paul Cook to visit and be interviewed on the air.

Klein sits down with the pair before airtime and tries explaining what words can and cannot be said over the air. "Curse all you want now," he says, "because you're going to be clean when you go into the studio. Say the dirty words now so when you go on the radio they're all used up." He asks them some innocuous questions to give them a sense of what the on-air interview will be like.

"He can't tell one drum from the other," Jones says of Cook. "I'm the best guitar player in the world. I'm tasty."

"Is this live?" Cook asks.

"No," Klein says. "Live is for later."

"Then you're connin' us," Jones responds.

Klein walks the pair through some station-identification spots, without much success. "This is the Outcaste Hour," Cook says. "Fuck me."

"Did I do all right?" Cook asks Klein.

"Let's try again," Klein says, scribbling.

"Don't put a fuckin' script in front of me, you cunt," Cook says.

"Then do something original," Klein says.

"No," Cook says. "What more do you want?"

"What the fuck do I have this on for?" Jones asks as he pulls off his headphones and stomps on them. He tries to stand up but can't balance himself, so he falls back in his chair and tries to negotiate himself through a station-identification blurb.

"You're very drunk and you don't know what you're sayin'," Cook says.

"I'm very drunk and I don't know what I'm sayin'," Jones regurgitates.

"Now try to do it without Paul's help," Klein prods.

"Now try to do it without Paul's help," Jones repeats.

Davis enters the room and calls Klein aside. "Howie," he whispers. "Those creeps smeared snot all over the wall of the men's room."

Klein chuckles. "That's punk rock, Norman. Let's do a radio show."

"Who knows what may happen tonight?" Davis asks as he goes on the air. He lets a drunk Cook and an even drunker Jones play disk jockey: They pick the Ronettes' "Baby I Love You." So far so good.

Davis wonders aloud where Rotten and Vicious are.

"They were scared to go by airplane so they went by bus," says Cook.

"They've done too many interviews already. We locked 'em up back at the hotel," Jones counters.

No sooner are Cook and Jones on the air that the expletives start flying. Davis tosses off a disclaimer but it's too late.

"Bollocks! Bollocks!" cries Jones.

"You can say that here, man," says Klein. "They don't know what 'bollocks' means over here."

"Fuck you, man," says Cook, imitating Klein's delivery.

"Don't say 'fuck'," Klein shoots back.

Davis cues the Stooges' "Lost Planet Boy," but Jones fiddles with the speed knob on the turntable until what goes out on the air is completely unclear. Davis eventually wrestles control away.

"Some people call Iggy Pop the godfather of punk," Davis says after he fades out the song.

"I'd call him a big toss-pot," contends Jones.

Then Davis lets the show get completely out of control.

"You must be a Pakistani," Jones says to the first, insecure caller.

"Fuck you. You must be full of shit," Jones says to the second caller.

"Punk rockers don't do drugs," Davis informs the third caller.

"Are you deaf or what!" Jones shouts at the fourth caller.

"I'm eleven years old," comes the slight voice of the fifth caller.

"I'm interested," Jones says.

The calls deteriorate even further.

"What are you on?" one caller asks.

"We're on the fuckin' radio! What do you think we're on?!"

Jones picks the New York Dolls' "Who Are the Mystery Girls" and Davis uses the time off the air to reclaim order.

"I've got a question for the Sex Pistols, man."

"Go ahead," Davis intones.

"My friend says blond cunt hairs are better and I say—"

"Next call."

The show hits its nadir when Jones turns it into his personal dial-a-date. When a woman calls, his first question is "Do you have big tits?" and then gets progressively more graphic.

This goes on for the better part of an hour. Jones and Cook proposition women over the phone, make fun of certain San Francisco suburbs at Klein's prodding, and attack everything they can think of. No useful information is offered (except when Jones, chatting up a woman over the air, tells her to meet him at the Miyako), but everyone has a good time.

Everyone, that is, except for certain citizens of the slandered suburbs who are outside waiting for Jones and Cook to leave the studio. The KSAN studios are on the outskirts of San Francisco's financial district, so at night it's very isolated. Anything can happen.

On their way to Klein's 1962 Ford Fairlane, Steve and Paul are met by half a dozen young men from Hayward.

"Why you fuckin' with our town?" one asks.

The initial attacks are vocal, but they soon escalate into mild shoving. Steve, Paul, and Boogie are drunk and want to fight.

Klein tries to defuse the situation. "Come on, men. Let's show them how great America is. Let's show them that we can take it."

The group moves backward toward Klein's car, moving

extremely slowly at first and gradually breaking into a quick trot. The band members jump into the car and Klein floors it. As they pass the parking lot, Boogie opens his car door and knocks down one of the Hayward greasers.

"They'll remember us, all right," Cook says, and grins wide.

4 A.M.

Two teenagers dodge street lights on the side of Winterland, the site of the Sex Pistols show, only sixteen hours away. They take their spray cans out of their jackets and go to work. They paint NEGATIVE TREND! in black on the side of Winterland and crawl off into the pre-dawn.

Johnny stares down the Tulsa crowd while Steve attends to other matters.

Sid and Paul pose; Johnny and Glen enjoy a Polaroid.

Later the same day, the miles have taken their toll.

ROBERTA BAYLEY

Steve and Malcolm in
San Francisco, on the
outside looking in

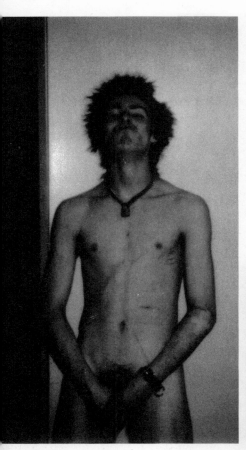

Sid before . . .

. . . and after his California bathing,
here with Glen Allison,
director of delousing

The crew

Johnny goes shopping in
San Francisco's Chinatown

Sid scowls and Johnny pouts during the tour's only radio interview.

KSAN's Bonnie Simmons tries to give Sid direction.

This is a rare photo of Malcolm listening to someone else, in this case San Francisco promoter Bill Graham.

ROBERTA BAYLEY

ROBERTA BAYLEY

For their last waltz at the Winterland, the band members hardly notice one another's presence.

DATE	DESCRIPTION	AMOUNT
8014 5/1	Gross 21800.00	$66.00
	less split 21690.00	
	110.00	
	-6	
	% 66.00	
	Gtr. 1000.00	
	1066.00	
	less partial 1000.00	
	66.00	

The settlement stub for the Winterland show. The Sex Pistols played to more than 5,000 people. They got paid $66.00.

End of the Road. Johnny and Noel look beaten the day after the San Francisco show.

CHAPTER FOURTEEN

Day Twelve: Saturday, January 14—San Francisco

6 A.M.

WIRED FROM CLUB-HOPPING and half-zonked from fatigue, Johnny Rotten and Sid Vicious pull into their last American truckstop.

Vicious looks out the front bus window. "Motorcycle out there, mates. Truckstop for us."

Vicious, who has crabs, has crawled into Monk's bunk a few hours ago while Monk was settling the tab at the Roxy. As a result, Sid has infected Monk and his belongings. Needless to say, Monk is not amused.

"There goes another franchise," D.W. chuckles.

"I'm ready for my steak and eggs," Vicious tells Monk as he gets off the bus.

"Have anything you want," Monk responds. "Just don't touch me or anything that belongs to me. Glen and I are going to stay back in the bus. D.W. is going to keep an eye on you. Don't give him any shit."

"No problem," Sid says.

Noel and Glen crawl into their respective bunks. Just as they are about to catch up on some long-overdue REM, they hear the sound of D.W. banging his fist against the door of the bus.

"You'd both better get up now," D.W. says after Monk and Allison reach the door. "Sid's not making many friends."

If the imposing D.W. needs help keeping matters in line, this crew has a big problem.

D.W. brings Monk and Allison over to the truckstop. In one booth, Rotten sits by himself, sneezing into the sleeve of his plaid jacket. D.W., Monk, and Allison sit down in his booth.

At the booth next to him, Sid sits alone. He's facing the next booth, filled with two cowboys and their girlfriends.

A black trucker walks past the tables. Vicious reaches between booths, nudges the cowboy next to him, and shouts, "That nigger is as good as any white guy."

One of the cowboys looks at Sid in his leather jeans and chain-collar and asks, "What do you know? What do you do for a living, funny-looking?"

"I'm a fuckin' guitar player!" Sid grins.

"You don't even have a real job," the cowboy says, and stands up on the other side of the booth. "You think you're a tough guy, huh?"

Sid cries, "Yeah!"

"Well, where's your fucking guitar, boy?"

"Up yer ass!"

The cowboy turns red. He snarls, "So you guys are the Sex Pistols. You're a bunch of tough motherfuckers, huh? What are you doing in America? What do you like to fuck?"

Sid answers, "I like to fuck boys, girls, dogs, I don't give a shit. As long as I can fuck it, that's OK with me."

No laughter.

The cowboy says, "You think you're a fuckin' tough guy," and puts out a cigarette on the back of his hand. His girlfriend frowns at him. The cowboy stares at Sid and beckons, "Come on, punk."

Everyone braces; Sid does not back down from a direct challenge. He stops eating his rare steak and runny eggs, picks up his steak knife and slashes the back of his left hand twice, deep.

The blood drips down his fingers and arm and makes his eggs even runnier. The cowboys look at each other and know they'll never one-up that one. The crew smiles; even Johnny enjoys a smirk. Sid finishes his food; the waitress asks all of them to leave.

"Excuse me," Monk says. "These men need their nourishment." Sid dashes for the bathroom.

10 A.M.

The tour bus pulls into the Cavalier Motel, a slum pit near the San Francisco Airport. Malcolm has checked into the Miyako, a beautiful hotel downtown, with Rory, Steve, and Paul. The crew hears that when Steve and Paul flew with Malcolm and Rory to San Francisco, they caused a commotion. A big stir on the plane, Rotten thinks. Malcolm must be making press again. Pathetic.

As Monk enters his room, he picks up a ringing phone.

"Finally!" Carl Scott shouts into the phone. "Where have you guys been? I thought you were dead until I heard you made a mess at the Roxy."

"Oh yeah," Monk says, as if he's just realized that he hasn't talked to anyone from the record company since Tulsa. "Sorry about that." He's not really sorry, but the free-lancer must act like he wants to keep his employer happy.

"We'll deal with this later," Scott says. "Right now you'd better call up Malcolm, because he wants to talk to Johnny something bad."

Scott doesn't say if McLaren is angry that two of his prized possessions have disappeared for a few days, but it's reasonable to assume that McLaren had been complaining about Monk since Monk pinned him to the wall by his lapels. The FBI incident probably hadn't brought them closer together, either.

1 P.M.

"I'm serious," says Roberta Bayley. "You've got to tell me how you're going to pay me. Do you really have the money?"

Forcade shifts uncomfortably in his seat and stands up. "Relax, relax. All in good time." He paces the Miyako room.

"You're a fine photographer and we will use your work and compensate you for your time. You will be paid."

"How, Tom? How?"

"You don't think I'm good for it?" Tom walks across the room and stands on the edge of his hotel-room bed, next to his open suitcase.

"I'm worried, Tom. I'm broke."

Forcade reaches into his suitcase, grabs a five-pound bar of gold, and holds it chest-high for Bayley to see. "You see this?"

"Yeah."

"If you're worried about the money," Forcade says, "Take that." He tosses it across the room at her; it sails past her, smashes against the window sill and falls to the floor. "Come on. If you want it, take it."

Bayley is too freaked out to pick it up. She doesn't know if Forcade will let her out of the room with it.

2 P.M.

After a short, fitful kip, Rotten and Vicious travel to a radio interview at KSAN, the only interview they've agreed to do on the entire tour. Rotten and Vicious have agreed to be interviewed. But not without a concession.

"Bonnie Simmons is a major deejay and you're going to have to be nice," Monk says in the cab from the hotel to the radio station. "I know you don't want to be, but it would really be helpful."

"Let me make it easy for you," Ted Cohen offers. He is reunited with the band and crew after his Dallas scare. "If you do this interview, I'm going to buy you both brand-new leather jackets."

"Got yourself a deal, mate," Vicious says.

"You're not going to buy us any bloody leather jackets," Rotten scoffs.

"Trust me," Cohen asserts.

When the group enters KSAN's control room, Bonnie Simmons looks severe. "Steve and Paul pulled some real shit on us last night," she tells Monk. "If that's going to happen again, I'd rather not do the interview."

"Don't worry," Monk says. "Everything will be in line."

"OK," Simmons says, and turns to Rotten and Vicious, who are sitting away from the control console in front of microphones. "When we have artists over, we let them play anything they want to. Steve and Paul did that last night. If you want to, let me know what you want to play and we'll play it."

Sid picks up a record and tosses it at Simmons. "Put this on, bitch."

"Suit yourself," Simmons says and puts on her headphones, ready to start the interview.

"Sid, do me a favor," Monk says as he pushes the palm of his right hand into the back of Vicious's neck. "Can you act half-human for one minute? This is a nice lady over here. Besides, there's a brand-new leather jacket waiting for you if you do this right."

Vicious calms down. "I'd better get that jacket," he says.

Simmons goes on the air and introduces Rotten and Vicious, both of whom slump in their chairs and ignore her.

"Have you been having fun?" Simmons asks, hopeful that someone will answer.

"Yeah," Vicious says. "It's been great, especially when they throw beer cans at us."

Rotten mumbles, "It's all a bunch of bollocks" in the background, almost inaudible.

"Well," Simmons, sizing up the situation. "Should I play another cut from your album?"

"Go ahead," Vicious says. "I don't give a —"

"Well, OK," Simmons interrupts. "Here we go."

By the time they're back live on the air, the band members are more agreeable.

"They're gonna buy us a leather jacket," Rotten says.

"They're gonna buy us some good things," Vicious claims.

Rotten interrupts Vicious before he can tell the KSAN audience what those good things are. "I want my leather jacket already."

"Keep going," Monk says off-mike. "I'll tell you when you earn it."

"No one tells us what to do," Vicious declares.

"Yes they do," Rotten counters, deadpan. "For a leather jacket I'd sell my soul."

Vicious babbles on a bit, barely decipherable, about sex on the road.

"Oh come on already," Rotten says off-mike. "I say I deserve a leather jacket."

"You deserve two sleeves," Monk says. "Keep going."

"Bloody hell," Rotten responds.

"I guess it's time to go to another song," Simmons says.

"Please, can we leave?" Rotten implores off the air. "This is unbelievably tedious."

"Nope," Monk announces. "Keep going."

When the music's over, Simmons tries again to approximate an interview, asking them about new material. This is a sore spot for Rotten—the band as a working, writing unit is long dead—so he keeps his mouth shut.

"We're getting new material all the time," Vicious lies. He says they've just written songs about South Africa (about "how the niggers are gonna rise up") and God ("It's a real attack. It's a death march.").

"I've had more fun on this tour than any other tour," he adds, then injects more candor. "I've had a chance to straighten up."

Instead of pursuing this line of questioning, Simmons busies herself with reading the mandated hourly ID statement. "Blah blah," Vicious and Rotten chant in the background like it's a demonic children's singsong.

"I want to say something," Vicious announces after letting Rotten say how much he hates everything.

"Well go ahead," Simmons allows.

"I want to say hello to Dee Dee Ramone if he's listening."

"I don't think KSAN's signal reaches quite as far as New York," Simmons suggests. "Do you like the Ramones?"

"Yeah!" Sid shouts. "I love the Ramones."

The voice of unremitting cynicism returns. "I hate the Ramones," Rotten says. "I hate them. I hate them. They're boring and mundane."

"Well then who do you like?" Simmons asks.

"Me," Rotten answers.

"I would hope so," Simmons says. "Anybody else?"

"Not really, no. Not at all. I don't like rock music. I don't even know why I'm in it. It's just the only way I can destroy things. It's the best way."

Simmons changes the subject. "Tell me about your song 'New York.'"

"It's about impostors from New York, all those cheap assholes who call themselves poets and take themselves seriously and all they're doing is destroying music in a ridiculous way," Rotten says. "It's like they're taking it on a serious level. At least we're destroying it practically. I want to just ruin everything." Then, turning to the crew: "Have I earned my leather jacket? This is so tedious."

"This is hard, isn't it," Simmons says, nearly outdeadpanning Rotten.

"Yes," says Rotten, picking up the challenge. "For a young man like me."

Simmons reads a listing of the bands playing in town tonight, making clear how much an alternative the Sex Pistols are to the likes of Grover Washington, Jr., She then tries to rekindle the talk.

"Are you going home after this show?" Simmons asks.

"As soon as our visas run out," Rotten says.

"So you are going home after that?"

"Well, we *have* to. We're being evicted out of your wonderful, free country. Think about that."

"You have to go back after a month?"

"Where are we going after this?" Sid asks John.

John ignores him and says, "A month? Try two weeks! Yeah, that's called your liberated country!"

"Yeah," Sid jumps in. "Real free!" Then, with unexplained derision: "President Carter."

"Your lovely stars and stripes," Rotten adds. If Rotten had done his homework, he'd know that he's spouting his unformed political ideas at a radio station whose format is in the hands of a group of disciplined Marxists.

"Every cowboy just looking for an excuse to blow you away," Vicious says. "Know what I mean? That's nowhere. Those people are nowhere. They're so big and tough and, like—"

Rotten interrupts. "What are you going on about, Sidney?"

Simmons tries again to wrestle some control. "Do you think it's different here than in England?"

Rotten leans into the microphone. "Yeah, all right. We thought we had problems, but comin' here looking at you people, my God! You're all so messed up. You're so like, lethargic! Your government is using you like puppets!"

Then the interview completely falls apart. "Go get your leather jackets," Simmons says.

"Finally," Rotten says. He and Vicious up and leave in a huff.

"Thanks," Simmons says as they're halfway out the door. The door shuts and she intones into the microphone, "Well, I think he heard me." She cues up another song and removes her headphones.

"Thanks for keeping them somewhat under control," she tells Monk and Cohen.

"No, they wanted to do it," Monk says. "They wouldn't have done it if they didn't want to."

"I'd hate to see what they'd be like if they didn't want to do it," Simmons says. "It's too bad they didn't want to play records. They could have had fun and relaxed. Oh well. Seeya at the gig."

Back in the car, Rotten asks Cohen, "Well, when are you going to give us our jackets?"

"Jackets?" Cohen mock-asks. "What jackets? Noel, did you hear about any jackets?"

Rotten spits, "I knew you were going to fucking welsh on us, you creepy record-company fuckhead."

Cohen smiles. "That'll pay you back for busting a lamp over my head, Johnny boy."

Monk takes the band members' side. "Teddy, you promised them, and I'm going to make good on your promise." He directs the car to a leather shop (actually, it's virtually a bondage shop) and buys them the finest, most expensive leather jackets he can find. He doesn't care about the expense; Warner Brothers will pick it up.

When he leaves the shop, Rotten throws his new jacket on the sidewalk and orders Monk, Vicious, and Cohen to jump on it. "It has to look worn," he says. "It has to. I don't want anything beautiful or new."

Just about the same time, Howie Klein is driving to the Miyako, where he hopes to interview McLaren and hang out with the band members. On the way to the hotel, he passes Winterland and a long ticket line. On the line, he sees members of Negative Trend, a local punk band Klein doesn't much care for. I hope they get tickets, Klein thinks. Maybe they'll learn something at the show.

3:30 P.M.

By the time Klein arrives at McLaren's room at the Miyako, he comes in on the tail end of a heated argument Malcolm and Bill Graham are having about the evening's opening bands.

Graham is the most successful and controversial rock-concert promoter in the country. He founded the Fillmore West in San Francisco and the Fillmore East in New York (Monk was a stage manager at the latter) and has acquired a reputation as a pit bull or cheap, depending on whether he's an ally or an adversary.

Graham's chosen sound is the psychedelic strain of San Francisco; mainstays at his halls have been Jefferson Airplane, the Grateful Dead, and Santana (whom he also manages), but he senses that punk might be the future and he doesn't want to be left behind.

Nonetheless, he has grave reservations about handling a Sex Pistols concert. When Premier Talent was booking the tour back in November, they passed on to Graham that it was McLaren's wish that the venues be limited to halls that seat less than one thousand.

"Is he serious about this?" Graham asks Bob Regehr at booking time.

Regehr nods. "Yup," he says into the phone.

Graham expresses to Regehr his great concerns about having the show in a small club. He cites security reasons, but Graham also suspects that he won't be able to make any money unless he books the Sex Pistols into a larger room. (He doesn't know yet how low ticket prices are going to be.)

"I don't want them playing a club," he says. "If they do, we both know there's going to be a major street problem. The Sex Pistols are very popular in San Francisco. There will be too many people outside the facility."

"I know," Regehr says. "I'll pass the word on to Malcolm."

Regehr calls a few hours later. "Sorry, Bill. No go."

Graham has had that time to prepare. "OK, Bob, try this. Today's what? Wednesday? Tell Malcolm that over the weekend I'll talk to KSAN. We're going to want them involved because they're the only ones in the country playing the damn record. I'll have them run a contest to see how many people want to go see the Sex Pistols."

"OK," Regehr says. "This had better work."

Regehr calls Graham back half an hour later. "Malcolm says fine. Good luck."

On Monday morning, Graham calls Regehr.

"We did it," Graham says.

"Well?"

"Why don't you go ask Malcolm what we're gonna do with forty-two hundred pieces of mail?"

"Great, Bill, great. I'll call you right back."

McLaren relays back to Graham that he's thrilled by the response. McLaren agrees to play Winterland, which has fifty-four hundred seats and offers a format in which Graham's security crew can maintain control. Winterland sells out in two days.

The only problem with this scenario is that Graham never called KSAN. He knew he could bluff his way into Winterland because no one from Warner Brothers was within KSAN's range. No one would know the query never went over the air.

"Sometimes the only way to get people to believe you is to be outlandishly crazy," Graham says.

But today Graham can't bluff much: McLaren is only two feet away from him.

"I've given you my final proposal," McLaren says. "Open microphone or no show."

"I'm not going to let every sick little punk shmuck in town on my stage," Graham says. "If you want an open microphone, I'm canceling the show. I'm not making anything on it anyhow. We'll talk about this tomorrow."

Graham storms out of the room.

"What was that about?" Klein asks McLaren after he introduces himself.

"I want someone to blow the Sex Pistols off the stage," McLaren says.

"The Pistols are great," Klein says. "What are you talking about?"

"We're turning into a rock band," McLaren says. "I hate rock bands. I want to make it all exciting again. I want a great band to come up there and wipe us into oblivion and make us start all over again. Make it street-level again."

"I don't think you're going to find a band in San Francisco that can do that," Klein says. "A lot of the bands here are really bad."

McLaren feels a smile coming. "Tell me, Howard. What's the worst band in San Francisco?"

Klein ponders for a moment. "Negative Trend. No question. It's Negative Trend. They're horrible."

"Can you find them?" McLaren inquires.

"Yeah. I saw them standing on line for tickets on the way over. What are you talking about?"

"You have to get them in touch with me," McLaren says. "They're the worst band in San Francisco. I want them to open up for the Sex Pistols."

6 P.M.

John Holmstrom and Roberta Bayley are being thrown out of the sound check.

"CIA! CIA!" Monk yells at them. "No CIA here! D.W., take 'em out!"

"What's your problem?" Holstrom asks. "We're just tryin' to do our job."

"The band doesn't want you here," Monk says.

"That sounds pretty strange to me," Bayley says. "Paul Cook gave me these tickets."

Monk turns to D.W. "Get 'em out of here." The paranoia maintains its fever pitch.

7 P.M.

Annie Leibovitz arrives at Winterland for a brief photo shoot, and she catches the band's ennui and frustration in four-color desperation. None of the four members is talking to each other; none of them is willing to pose for *Rolling Stone*. She chronicles the impending disintegration.

Winterland is the largest place the band has played in America by a factor of four. It's a major San Francisco theater. The punks are in the center of hippiedom. Graham's staff has opened the doors more than an hour earlier than usual to create a peaceful situation. To keep matters in hand, Graham has also seen to it that during the show the house lights will remain twenty percent lit. He arms the balcony and downstairs staffs with two-way radios. He also has someone near the main power switch. He is afraid of what the band members might suggest on stage (just as the vice squads did at the beginning of the tour). He fears liability and lawsuits. Graham likens his preparations for the show to "planning an invasion."

Three bands are set to perform tonight, according to the marquee: the Nuns, the Avengers, and then the Sex Pistols. During the Nuns' set, some of the punks in the front of the crowd toss syringes on stage.

Bill Graham turns to Monk stage right and says to his former employee, "If this is what rock and roll is coming to, I don't know if I want to be a part of it."

Next up are the Avengers, a local punk band led by Penelope Huston. (It's a mark of San Francisco's acceptance of punk that it's the only city that can come up with genuinely punk opening bands.)

The Avengers have been together since June 1977; they have an EP out on the independent Dangerhouse label. The Sex Pistols are important to them, but they're not trying to sound like them. Early on, before the singles of "God Save the Queen" and "Anarchy in the U.K." filtered into American specialty shops, nobody in America save the cognoscenti knew what was happening in England. But those looking knew *something* was happening, even if they didn't know what it was, so bands formed overnight. The Avengers are Huston's first band. Johnston saw them perform in Los Angeles, and he liked what he heard enough to put them on the bill for the Winterland show. Because they know Rory, they get the middle slot of the bill instead of the bottom.

When the Nuns, who have been around a little longer than the Avengers, discovered that they were going on before the Avengers, one of the band members called Huston.

"We're a bigger band than the Avengers," he said. "If you guys wanna trade slots with us, that's OK. We'll do that for you if you wanna do that." Huston declines the offer and laughs.

The Avengers are being paid a mere $250 to perform tonight, which Huston alludes to during one song. The words to one of the group's numbers, "I Believe in Me," change every time they play. Except for the chorus, Huston always makes up the lyrics on stage, on the spot.

Tonight one of the verses is: "You think we're doing this for money?/Well, we're not!/We're getting paid shit!" Bootleggers duly capture the outburst for posterity.

All the excitement during the Avengers' set isn't on stage. A hall security guard knocks on the door to Graham's office and tells his boss there's a problem backstage. "The Pistols and Malcolm are here," he says. "But so is a whole 'nother band, with all their equipment. Malcolm told me, 'These are friends of ours. We want them to go on before us. Tell the Yank we're not playing unless they go on before us.'"

"I guess I'm 'the Yank,'" Graham snickers.

"I guess so."

"Let's go backstage."

When Graham arrives backstage, the Sex Pistols have scattered but McLaren, the members of Negative Trend, and their equipment are waiting for him. This is the first show McLaren has attended. With Graham the field marshal, he knows this show will be safe.

Malcolm points to the extra musicians. "These are our friends, Negative Trend."

"Oh yeah," Graham says. "The spray-paint kids."

"That's revolution, Yank," McLaren says. "If you want a Sex Pistols show, Negative Trend must go on before them. Otherwise, I can't be held responsible for what happens."

Graham walks to within six inches of McLaren. "Are you asking or demanding?" he inquires, trying hard to contain his anger. "My man tells me that a threat was made. It's not wise to threaten."

As always happens when his confrontation is met by further confrontation (especially if it's met by someone bigger), McLaren backs down. "We're not demanding. We'd like them to play before us. We think they're very good."

Graham leaks a little smile. He has his opening. He says, "You may not agree with me, but that might cause a big problem. The public expected two groups and then the Pistols. If these guys go on stage before you, they will not be received well. They'll also be taking your time. For every song they do, there will be one less song that you'll do. It's not that I don't want them to play, that's not it. It's just that I think you'll be ill-advised to have them go on before you. But they can play after you, if you like. That would work in everybody's favor. The audience would get what was advertised, and then you can do what you want to do."

McLaren lifts his left forefinger to his mouth, ponders the ramifications for half a minute, then says. "All right. Maybe having Negative Trend go on before the Sex Pistols would work against both bands. I'd like to propose a compromise: Negative Trend goes on after the Sex Pistols."

"That sounds fair," Graham says. "I knew you were a reasonable man, Malcolm."

Graham shakes McLaren's hand and exits. On the way back to his office, he figures out how to be sure that the evening ends after the Sex Pistols' set.

10 P.M.

Emcee Richard Meltzer announces the Sex Pistols by riling up the audience. He incites the crowd to become something more than a passive American rock audience. He sets a tone that the band must live up to. "Skinheads suck!" he shouts. "You all suck dick!" Meltzer has stapled a Tampax box to the outside of his jacket. Graham has him ejected before he can finish his speech. After the security guards have thrown him out, Meltzer turns his jacket inside out and sneaks back in.

The Sex Pistols' set is an astonishing, galvanizing show for the Winterland audience. Although many in the crowd have seen punk bands before (the Ramones have already been through town twice), this opens the door to a new world. The sound is all Jones's buzzsaw chords and Rotten's invectives, noise, and anger. There's no hint that anything constructive could come out of this fury, just a sour-breathed, fire-breathing celebration of the power of destruction. There's a rousing dissolution on the stage, fury bathed in white spotlights.

Yet those on stage are neither astonished nor galvanized. The Winterland show is a blasé, seen-it-all show by a band that is tired, bored, sick. Rotten asks the sellout crowd, "A-ha! Ever have the feeling you've been cheated? Good night." The answer should be yes. This show, in comparison to the Texas shows, is dull beyond belief. Anarchy is a word that slides out of Rotten's mouth; tonight it doesn't mean anything.

As with the Dallas show, a crew commissioned by Warner Brothers is filming the gig. Regehr hired the crew and intends to pay for it himself. He feels he has spent enough company money on the Sex Pistols, but he wants to preserve the show for posterity. It's doubtful that anyone in the band knows how much he cares. To make sure the sound is acceptable, Boogie switches Sid's amp off.

KSAN is broadcasting the concert. Norman Davis and Bonnie Simmons offer preshow commentary backstage and in the crowd. Tonight's show will touch off a punk explosion in San Francisco, and because of the KSAN broadcast that inspiration will not be limited to those at Winterland. Besides, most of the ticket-holders aren't hard-core punks. This is the tour's only pot-smoking crowd, just curious to see what the hell these Sex Pistols are all about.

As the Sex Pistols wind down their encore, Graham prepares to make sure that Negative Trend never gets a chance to take his stage. McLaren has made preparations to have the

Sex Pistols' equipment taken off as soon as possible. Negative Trend's equipment is already on the side of the stage, so they can set up quickly and retain the audience.

What McLaren doesn't know is that Graham has encouraged a tradition to develop over the years at the halls he runs. When he receives a signal that the headliner has played his or her final encore, he would cue up Mason Williams's soft version of "Greensleeves" as a sign that the evening is over.

The second the Sex Pistols leave the stage, before the house lights come up, Graham motions the house sound mixer to play "Greensleeves." When the tape goes on, the crowd quickly empties. Within ten minutes, the hall is half-empty. Five minutes later, with only a small fraction of the audience still lingering, Negative Trend is ready to go on.

McLaren confronts Graham. "Where's the crowd? Why'd everyone go home?"

"It's all yours now, sweetheart," Graham says.

"That wasn't a nice thing to do," says McLaren. "How can I do a proper show without an audience?"

"You're right, Malcolm. It wasn't a nice thing to do. But it's not nice to threaten, either."

McLaren walks away in a huff, and Graham returns to a paper cup on his desk. After the Sex Pistols left the stage, he had walked on to pick up some of the debris. He turns the cup upside down on his desk, and chuckles at his collection of nuts, bolts, pins, coins, a pair of glasses, and one dirty sock.

Midnight

Not surprisingly, none of the Sex Pistols has shown up for the press reception. The Avengers must entertain the press. A line of photographers lays in wait, as do a dozen or so genuine punks who have weaseled backstage. A food fight ensues, popcorn butter on the floor, everyone slipping on it. Flash bulbs blind the Avengers. The photographers want punks, so the Avengers will act like punks. It's silly fun.

It's not fun in the Sex Pistols' private dressing room. Annie Leibovitz is trying to set up a shot of the Sex Pistols in a shower. Cooperation comes slowly.

Rotten and Cohen sit back on a couch and relax.

"What do you know?" Cohen says to Rotten. "San Francisco today. Brazil tomorrow."

"What?"

"You're going to Brazil tomorrow."

"What?"

"Don't you understand what I'm talking about?"

"What?"

Cohen explains the Biggs-Brazil scenario. "I was just talking to Steve and Paul about it. They said you were going tomorrow."

"I don't know what's going on here," Rotten says as he rises from his chair. "But I'm bloody well not gonna go to Brazil. And I promise you that Sidney's not going either. Now if you excuse me I have to go and find Malcolm so I can tell him to stuff it."

McLaren is nowhere to be found (he's off sulking about the Negative Trend fiasco), which enrages Rotten even more. "Where's that wanker?!" he screams.

He's not here, but McLaren's Machiavellian interests are well-served. Without McLaren having to bear the brunt of the attacks, the band members argue whether to go with McLaren to South America.

McLaren's goal for the South American jaunt is simple. Rotten is the only member of the band with a brain and a mouth that can rival his. He has to be extricated.

The band members scatter. Jones and Cook, faithful employees, agree to fly south. Rotten refuses to go and returns to the Cavalier Motel with Monk.

Sid is nowhere to be found. He has disappeared with Lamar, the groupie from Dallas who followed him here. By the time Monk finds out about Vicious's disappearance, it's too late for him to do anything about it.

2 A.M.

"Fuck it," Rotten tells Monk back at the Cavalier Motel. "Let's go to the Miyako. Maybe if I meet with the arsehole I can make sense of it."

"South America can be a dangerous situation," Monk says. "Think about it before you go."

"Don't worry," Rotten says, and smiles for the first time all night. "I'm not going to back up a train robber. Can you believe it: a bleedin' train robber?"

Monk and Rotten share a cab to the Miyako in silence. Rotten senses he's about to be sacked, but he's not going to go without raising a fuss.

As the pair walk into the lobby, Monk sees Bayley and Holmstrom and repeats his "CIA!" chant. They pay him no attention.

"Wait downstairs," Rotten says. "I have to do this m'self."

"Suit yourself." Monk retires to the hotel bar.

Rotten walks to the elevator and presses the button. The elevator door opens and out walks Van Morrison, the great Irish soul singer who also records for Warner Brothers. Morrison and Rotten stand next to each other and stare for a moment. They have common ground, but neither realizes or admits it. Morrison shakes his head and walks away.

Rotten meets Johnston and Boogie at the door to McLaren's room.

"The band is going to Brazil," Johnston says. "You have to go."

"It's the right thing to do, mate," Boogie says.

"I ain't goin'," Rotten says and pushes past them.

Rotten enters the room and sees Vicious, who has reappeared along with Lamar, arguing with McLaren.

"But I don't have any money to give you, Sidney," McLaren says. "I'm sorry."

"I need it," Vicious says. "I'm not asking for it. You'd better give it to me."

"I ain't got it."

"Fuck you then," Vicious says. He jumps atop the dresser and kicks out the mirror. Glass flies back at him but he doesn't care. Vicious stares at McLaren. "You're going to die for what you've done," he says and stalks out, Lamar by his side.

"Well then," McLaren says to those assembled in the room (the three remaining band members, Boogie, Sophie, and Johnston), brushing glass shards off his overcoat. "Anyone else want to play this foolish game or shall we plan how we are going to conquer Brazil?"

"Warner Brothers may not support us if we go to Brazil," Johnston says.

"Then we sack Warner Brothers," McLaren theorizes. "Virgin will pay the bills. We haven't begun to soak Branson yet."

"Warner Brothers wants us to go back to the East Coast, make up the beginning of the tour, and include New York," Johnston informs.

"Warner Brothers wants this," Jones says in a nyah-nyah voice. "Warner Brothers wants that."

"I'd like to see bloody New York," Cook says.

"We are not going to New York," McLaren shoots back. "Besides, don't we have a problem with visas, my friend?"

"We can stay a few more days," Johnston says. "And Jaffe can get us extensions. They want—"

"I don't bloody care what they want," McLaren interrupts. "They don't run this band. I do. And I say we're going to Brazil."

"This ain't your band," Rotten charges. He's slumping deep into the couch, saving all his energy for his hatred of McLaren. "You don't play out there. You don't get shit thrown at you every night. You don't write the fuckin' songs."

"We ain't been writin' that many songs ourselves, mate," belches Jones.

"We are going to Brazil," McLaren says, emphasizing each syllable by pointing at Rotten.

"You can't go without me," Rotten contends.

"You're just one member of the band, Johnny boy," McLaren says. "You can be replaced."

"Let's cut through all the shit," Rotten says. "That's what this has all been about, innit? Sackin' me."

"No one wants to sack you," McLaren says. "Come with us to Brazil and stay in the band."

"If you wanted me to go to Brazil, why didn't you tell me about it?"

"It was an oversight, my boy. Just a small oversight."

"You can shove the oversight," Rotten says. "I ain't goin'

anywhere with you lot." He leaves the room and slams the door behind him.

"I'm bloody well fed up and disgusted," Rotten tells Monk after he meets him in the bar. "The band is over."

3:30 A.M.

Howie Klein is at a late-starting party in the Haight district. He's been standing in front of a closet door for twenty minutes. Although the loud hippie music engulfs the room, he thinks he hears a noise inside the closet. He opens the door and sees Sid Vicious on the floor, half-unconscious and moaning.

CHAPTER FIFTEEN

Sunday
January 15—End of
the Road

The way is dark
Night is long
I don't care if I ever get home
I'm waiting
At the end of the road

—Jerry Lee Lewis

11 A.M.

RORY AND BOOGIE HAVE found Sid. After a brief meeting with
Rotten at the Cavalier ("I ain't goin'," Rotten said between
sniffles. "Don't waste yer breath."), they go back to the Miyako
and find two of the kids who seemed to be following Sid and
Lamar last night. They get Lamar's address.

They arrive at Lamar's apartment seconds after Sid has
injected heroin into himself. The needle dangles from his
arm. Thanks to a controlled situation over the past week,
Vicious had been able to take his first tentative steps away
from his addiction. Without supervision, he has quickly returned to the poison.

But now's not the time to scold or theorize. Either the
smack hit is massive or Sid's body has lost some of its tolerance

because Sid has just collapsed onto the floor. His face is turning blue; he's unconscious and he's having trouble breathing.

Rory falls into a brief panic—so this is how the tour is going to end, he thinks—but quickly gains his bearings. He and Boogie get Sid on his feet and walk him around the room. After a few minutes, Sid is semiconscious and breathing normally.

"You stay here with Sid," an exhausted, exasperated Johnston tells Boogie. "I'm going to call Malcolm and find a doctor. I think some guy in Bill Graham's office knows an acupuncturist. Maybe he can help. Why don't you have Sid call Monk at the Cavalier? Give him someone to talk to."

"Noel or Sidney?"

"Just make the call."

Johnston leaves and Boogie calls Monk.

"Monk!" Vicious shouts into the phone. "I'm having a fucking great time! All right!"

"That's good, Sid. Where are you?"

"Lamar's house. She lives in San Francisco."

Lamar pulls the phone away from Sid and sounds close to tears. "Noel, what am I going to do with Sid? He's wrecking my record collection. He's trashing my apartment. I don't know what to do with him."

"Is he having a good time?"

"He's throwing up all over the place. He's having a great time. He's doing whatever he wants."

Noel smiles. "What more could you ask for? Have a good time, Lamar. It's been a lot of fun. Bye. Put Sid on."

"Hey, Monk!"

"Are you gonna take care of yourself?"

"Yeah, yeah, don't worry."

"Are you gonna call me when you get to New York?"

"Yeah, yeah, don't worry. I'll call you." Sid pauses, then says, "Hey, Monk."

"Yes, Sid?"

"Thanks for everything."

6 P.M.

Rotten has spoken to McLaren on the phone today about twenty times. The screaming is louder each time.

"It just goes from one circus to another," Rotten tells McLaren. "I'm not interested anymore." He slams the phone for the last time.

Monk, who can hear the screaming from his room next door, has been waiting in his hotel room all day to find out what happens next. Is the tour over? Is the band over?

Carl Scott calls and delivers the death knell. "The band is having major problems with McLaren," he says.

"No kidding," Monk deadpans.

"Listen, Noel. I don't know what's happening anymore, but the tour is over. Get in the bus. Get your crew. Go home. Say good-bye."

Monk has a farewell dinner in Chinatown with Rotten, who is unsure about what to do next except that it will have nothing to do with McLaren. "Bloody poseur. Let him take the sidemen down to that wanker in Rio. It doesn't bloody matter. Rory says he can get me into the Miyako now. I'll stay there for a few days and see what happens."

"Well, that's it," Monk says in front of the bus after dropping Rotten off at the Miyako. Rotten gives Monk a present, a badge with his picture on it. "Everything is slipping through my fingers," Johnny says. "This isn't the way it was supposed to end."

11 P.M.

After several hours of watching his house get trashed by a junkie rock star on what was supposed to be a quiet, comfortable Sunday evening, the acupuncturist throws Sid Vicious out of his house.

"Get him out of here," he tells Johnston. "There's nothing I can do for him."

Johnston plans to take Sid to a clinic in Los Angeles,

Johnston's adopted hometown, clean up the kid, and get him on a plane to London.

"When's the next gig?" Sid asks on the way out. He doesn't realize what has happened.

Rotten is lost and depressed, wondering who's going to pay his hotel bill. Vicious is lost in smack, unaware that he's out of a job. Jones and Cook, however, are having a ball.

Howie Klein has brought the pair down to KSJO in San Jose, where he hosts another punk show. It's an hour's drive from the Miyako.

As with the show he does on KSAN with Norman Davis, Klein has labeled his late-night slot the *Outcaste Hour*. KSJO is a more traditional, straight-ahead rock station than KSAN, so he gets much less leeway on the air. One woman on the staff, Kate Ingram, is assigned to stick around and make sure things don't get out of control.

She shouldn't have bothered. Since KSAN let them get away with their nonsense two nights earlier, Cook and Jones can't be reined in. They curse incessantly, beg for women to sleep with them, and slander everything they can think of.

Half an hour into the show, one woman hanging around the station takes Jones up on his offer. They disappear.

Klein asks Cook a few questions that yield the expected answers. Six minutes into this segment, Cook looks around the control room, bewildered. "Where's Steve? Go get Steve. Is he with that bird? I bet he's with that bird. Please get him back here. I can't be expected to entertain the audience all by myself. I'm just the fucking drummer."

EPILOGUE
Where Are They Now?

The Avengers were briefly managed by Rory Johnston, during which time they recorded an album produced by Steve Jones.

Penelope Huston was disillusioned by the Sex Pistols' Winterland show. "We were a pretty sincere kind of band, so it was shocking to see how the Sex Pistols acted. If they were supposed to represent punk, they were doing it in the worst possible way by being rock stars. People were idolizing them, and that's not what they wanted. They weren't leading anyone anywhere." She characterizes Jones as a "lecherous, dumb guy who didn't mean any harm." Huston continues as a solo act.

Dan Baird, the Atlanta fan, leads the Georgia Satellites. "There's music that comes brain first," Baird says. "And there's music that comes gut first. The Pistols definitely came gut first. They came in the long line of the tradition. Johnny Rotten and Johnny Burnette came from the same line. They've been looking at the back end of a mule; they want to rock." In their own way, the Georgia Satellites are also part of that broad, rich tradition.

Doreen Cochran managed the Atlanta band the Brains and eventually got tired of "dealing with useless record-company people on cocaine who'd fly into town to see the Brains and

who were too busy chasing pussy all night to watch the band."
She now does specialty construction work.

Paul Cook is back in England, drumming for the band Chiefs
of Relief. He served as a "technical adviser" for Alex Cox's
stylized film about Sid Vicious and the Sex Pistols, *Sid and
Nancy.*

Jim Dickinson remains a leading record producer. His most
lasting album of recent years is the Replacements' *Pleased To
Meet Me,* a raucous, triumphant record that's equal parts Rolling Stones, Sex Pistols, and Alex Chilton.

The **Great South East Music Hall** in Atlanta is now an office-
supplies warehouse.

Bill Goffrier was so inspired by the Tulsa show that he helped
form the Embarrassment, Middle America's finest punk unit.
In 1981, the Embarrassment opened up a Chicago show for
Rotten's new band, Public Image Limited. He now lives in
Boston and plays guitar for Big Dipper.

After the tour, **John Holmstrom** traveled to Jamaica with
Tom Forcade to find Johnny Rotten (who was there with Virgin chief Richard Branson, scouting new reggae talent) and
get him under Forcade's wing. Holmstrom also drew the
covers of *Rocket to Russia* and *Road to Ruin,* which turned out
to be the Ramones' strongest albums. He maintains that the
way the Sex Pistols tour was handled exemplifies much of
what is wrong in the way the entertainment industry deals
with drug abuse. "Sid Vicious was a heroin addict. He needed
medical attention. The problem of rock stars and drugs has
always been there. After thirty years of rock stars dying of
drug overdoses, record companies should have come up with
a more enlightened way of handling drug addiction other
than hiring someone to watch Sid twenty-four hours a day to
make sure he doesn't seek self-treatment. It's just a reflection
of how society treats the drug problem. Instead of getting Sid
the help he needed, Warner Brothers just made sure that he

didn't do anything they considered bad." Holmstrom is now executive editor of *High Times.*

Rory Johnston held out hope that the Sex Pistols would reunite and continued to work for Malcolm until the end of 1978, when McLaren's money ran out. He now manages Euphorbia Productions, which he owns along with Philip Glass.

Steve Jones followed Sid Vicious into junkiedom. He is now a member of Alcoholics Anonymous and does anti-drug commercials for MTV. He lives in California and is a recording artist for MCA Records. He has written songs with Andy Taylor (ex-Duran Duran) and "big toss-pot" Iggy Pop. He was last seen playing celebrity-baseball games and coaxing far more popular performers who owe some debt to his ancient band to sing old Sex Pistols B-sides on his records: He still can't sing lead. A dozen years after the Sex Pistols broke up, he still markets himself primarily as an ex-Sex Pistol.

When the Kingfish closed down, **Jim Rink** and his friend Don Spicer stole the club's power cords, figuring that possession of equipment the Sex Pistols once used would be a good omen.

Howie Klein got fired the day after the KSJO broadcast. "There haven't been so many complaints in the history of the station," the program director said. "The community was outraged." The program director was a friend of Klein's (he was in a punk band called Nuclear Valdez) but the general manager ordered him to fire Klein. The program director concocted a fake firing and rehiring within a month. The KSJO broadcast turned up on a bootleg called *Big Tits over America.* Klein ran the independent label 415 and is now an executive for Sire Records.

The **Longhorn** remains one of Dallas's preeminent country-and-western bars. The Sex Pistols show that Warner Brothers filmed there has never been officially released because it is unusable. The folks at Sun West Productions who shot the show

incorrectly synchronized the cameras, so editing was too tedious for Warner Brothers to pursue.

Negative Trend did get better, developing into Flipper, one of
San Francisco's longer-lasting punk bands, best known for
their song "Sex Bomb." The only lyrics to the song are "Sex
bomb/My baby, yeah!" The track is nearly eight minutes long.

Within days of seeing the Sex Pistols and having Johnny Rotten ignore him, **Mike Peters** and a friend started their own
punk band, the Toilets, which turned into Seventeen—named
after the Sex Pistols song—and finally, in 1982, the Alarm.
Their 1986 hit, "Spirit of '76," is punk's grandest elegy.

Bob Regehr continued to shepherd startling new talent: Who
else would have let performance artist Laurie Anderson release a five-album live set? He died of cancer in 1984. He was
fifty-two.

Johnny Rotten was briefly forgotten and abandoned in San
Francisco. His belongings were inadvertently left on the tour
bus and never returned. It took Warner Brothers a week to
bail him out of the Miyako. He then flew back to New York
and stayed with photographer Joe Stevens. When British journalist Caroline Coon asked him if there was any chance that
the Sex Pistols might reunite, he said, "I won't work with any
of them. Steve can go off and be Peter Frampton. Sid can go
off and kill himself and nobody will care. Paul can go back to
being an electrician. Malcolm will always be a Wally." He re-
verted to his Christian name John Lydon when he left the
band and founded the band Public Image Limited with junkie
guitarist Keith Levene, who had been fired from the Clash.
Lydon has recorded throughout the eighties, offering up
some of the most abrasive music around (1981's *Second Edition*,
parts of 1986's *album*), and some of the dumbest (everything
else). For Public Image Limited's first American performance,
at the Ritz in August 1981, the group refused to emerge from
behind a screen and caused a riot. He is married (to the
mother of Arri Up, member of the Slits) and he has had his
teeth fixed. In 1989, he said, "I don't recognize the impor-

tance of the Pistols anymore. It's gone, it's over. The only people interested in the Sex Pistols are yuppies, because *Never Mind the Bollocks* is finally available on CD. It fits very cozily between John Denver and Barry Manilow." As for Sid, he said, "I still feel quite sad about that. I should have put more effort in stopping his overindulgence instead of washing my hands of it. I regret not having done more for him." In 1986 he told Jimmy, "Everybody wants me to start the Sex Pistols Part Two or something like that, but I've got to keep moving forward. Anyway, a new band like the Sex Pistols isn't even necessary at this point. I'm waiting for something new, but I'm not going to do it. I've already done my bit, you know."

Soupy Sales's kids, bassist **Tony** and drummer **Hunt**, recovered from playing with Sid and later performed briefly with David Bowie as part of his Tin Machine band.

The **Taliesyn Ballroom** in Memphis is now a Taco Bell.

Rory brought **Sid Vicious** to a Los Angeles clinic and then put Boogie and him on a plane to New York, where they'd change planes and go to London. At the Los Angeles clinic, Sid was given enough methadone to get him through for two days, but he took it all at once when he got on the plane. He overdosed during the flight and spent a few days at Jamaica Hospital before Warner Brothers' Liz Rosenberg got him on a flight to London. The hospital told reporters that Sid was suffering from "nervous exhaustion." In London, Vicious reunited with Nancy Spungen and their shared addiction. Vicious recorded an indifferent solo album, appeared in the films *Mondo Video* and *The Great Rock and Roll Swindle,* and along with Spungen sank deeper into heroin addiction. They moved to New York, but Spungen never did have her wart removed. On October 12, 1978, she was killed in the couple's room at the Chelsea Hotel. Sid was arrested for the murder. On Groundhog Day 1979, while out on bail, he died of a heroin overdose, spawning a sick death cult of fans who found something enticing in his swift self-destruction. Sid was twenty-one.

Malcolm McLaren bailed Sid out of jail in October 1978, flew back to London, and started selling T-shirts with Sid's picture under the caption I'M ALIVE, SHE'S DEAD, I'M YOURS. He has continued to exploit the Sex Pistols name, with a film *The Great Rock and Roll Swindle* and half a dozen nearly identical albums. He managed Adam and the Ants and Bow Wow Wow and eventually decided he was a legitimate recording artist himself. He was wrong. He recorded four albums in which he took different forms of traditional or genre music, rerecorded and remixed them, and claimed writer's credit on them all. After a deal with CBS Films fell apart when the unit folded, he signed a seven-album deal with CBS Records.

Tom Forcade went into a deep depression when the Sex Pistols broke up. He told friends that they were the last chance for real anarchy in the U.S. and was profoundly disappointed that he never became a real part of them. On November 16, 1978, he walked to the bedroom of his Manhattan apartment, pointed a .45 at his head, and pulled the trigger. He died the next day.

The Sex Pistols became establishment. Only in their demise did they become safe. A small industry of bootlegs and paraphernalia continues unabated. Thousands of bands, from Billy Idol to Guns N' Roses, have been influenced by their music or their image. Popular American heavy-metal bands like Metallica frequently record versions of Sex Pistols songs. In 1986, the film *Sid and Nancy* became a cult hit; it remains the most popular theatrical film on American college campuses. In January 1988, ten years after the Sex Pistols broke up, their LP *Never Mind the Bollocks, Here's the Sex Pistols* was certified gold, and Warner Brothers, which had lost more than $200,000 on the band's American tour, issued a compact disk version. The same month, the three surviving Sex Pistols finally won a drawn-out lawsuit against McLaren for back publishing royalties. They each received more than £200,000. In early 1989, at the height of rock-reunion fever, Danny Heaps, Lydon's manager, was offered $2 million to bring the surviving Sex Pistols back together for a reunion tour. So far there have been no takers.

In little more than a year, the Sex Pistols recorded some of the most thrilling music in all rock and roll. Not even the vast amount of cynical exploitation that has arisen in their wake can ever undermine that.

Bibliography

Bangs, Lester. *Psychotic Reactions and Carburetor Dung: An Anthology.* (New York: Knopf, 1987).

Bromberg, Craig. *The Wicked Ways of Malcolm McLaren.* (New York: Harper & Row, 1988).

Burchill, Julie, and Tony Parsons. *The Boy Looked at Johnny: The Obituary of Rock and Roll.* (London: Faber and Faber, 1978).

Coon, Caroline. *1988: The New Wave Punk Rock Explosion.* (Menasha, Wis.: Omnibus, 1982).

Cox, Alex, and Abbe Wool. *Sid and Nancy: Love Kills.* (London: Faber and Faber, 1986).

Flippo, Chet. *It's Only Rock 'n' Roll.* (New York: St. Martin's, 1989).

Frith, Simon. *Sound Effects.* (New York: Pantheon, 1981).

Frith, Simon, ed. *Facing the Music.* (New York: Pantheon, 1988).

Frith, Simon, and Howard Horne. *Art into Pop.* (New York: Routledge, Chapman and Hall, 1987).

Hebdige, Dick. *Subculture: The Meaning of Style.* (New York: Methuen, 1979).

Hebdige, Dick. *Cut 'n' Mix: Culture, Identity and Caribbean Music.* (New York: Routledge, Chapman and Hall, 1987).

Marcus, Greil. *Lipstick Traces: A Secret History of the Twentieth Century.* (Cambridge, Mass: Harvard University Press, 1989).

Morris, Dennis. *Rebel Rock.* (Menasha, Wis.: Omnibus, 1985).

Nabokov, Vladimir. *Despair.* (New York: Putnam, 1966).

Reid, Jamie, and Jon Savage. *Up They Rise: The Unfinished Works of Jamie Reid.* (London: Faber and Faber, 1987).

Rimmer, Dave. *Like Punk Never Happened.* (London: Faber and Faber, 1985).

Stevenson, Ray, ed. *Sex Pistols File.* (Menasha, Wis.: Omnibus, 1978).

Sussman, Elizabeth, ed. *On the Passage of a Few People Through a Rather Brief Moment in Time.* (Cambridge, Mass.: MIT Press, 1989).

Taylor, Paul, ed. *Impresario: Malcolm McLaren and the British New Wave.* (Cambridge, Mass.: MIT Press, 1988).

Vermorel, Fred, and Judy Vermorel. *Sex Pistols: The Inside Story.* (Menasha, Wis.: Omnibus, 1987).

Wood, Lee. *Sex Pistols Day by Day.* (Menasha, Wis.: Omnibus, 1988).

Young, Scott. *Neil and Me.* (Toronto: McClelland and Stewart, 1984).

ABOUT THE AUTHORS

Noel Monk was stage manager at the Fillmore East and Woodstock. In the seventies, he worked in both America and Europe for the likes of the Rolling Stones, Johnny Cash, and the Moody Blues. He was personal manager for the enormously successful hard-rock band Van Halen from 1978 to 1985. He and his wife live in Southern California.

Jimmy Guterman writes for a variety of publications, among them *Rolling Stone, Esquire,* and *Spy.*

Noel and Jimmy are currently collaborating on a second book.